Virginia County Records

Volume VII

EDITED BY

William Armstrong Crozier

CLEARFIELD

Originally Published As
Virginia County Records
Volume VII
The Genealogical Association
Hasbrouck Heights, New Jersey, 1909

Reprinted
Genealogical Publishing Company
Baltimore, 1971

Reprinted for
Clearfield Company by
Genealogical Publishing Co.
Baltimore, Maryland
1993, 1994, 2000, 2008

Library of Congress Catalogue Card Number 67-29835
ISBN-13: 978-0-8063-0470-0
ISBN-10: 0-8063-0470-7

Made in the United States of America

The publisher gratefully acknowledges
the loan of the original of this book
by the
George Peabody Branch
Enoch Pratt Free Library
Baltimore, Maryland

Vol. VII　　　　　MARCH, 1910　　　　　Part 1

𝔙𝔦𝔯𝔤𝔦𝔫𝔦𝔞
ℭ𝔬𝔲𝔫𝔱𝔶 𝔕𝔢𝔠𝔬𝔯𝔡𝔰

PUBLISHED QUARTERLY

EDITED BY

William Armstrong Crozier, F. R. S., F. G. S. A.

Published by
The Genealogical Association
Hasbrouck Heights
New Jersey

Five Dollars a Year　　　　　Single Copies, Two Dollars

𝔙𝔦𝔯𝔤𝔦𝔫𝔦𝔞 𝔊𝔬𝔲𝔫𝔱𝔶 𝔕𝔢𝔠𝔬𝔯𝔡𝔰

Published Quarterly

CONTENTS

Virginia County Records

QUARTERLY MAGAZINE

| VOL. VII | MARCH 1910 | No. 1 |

INDEX TO LAND GRANTS
ACCOMAC COUNTY

Book No. 6

34	Stephen Barnes	1666	600
34	Christopher Thompson	1666	500
35	Robert Richardson	1666	2000
35	Thomas Selby	1666	1250
35	Alex. Williams	1666	600
36	Robert Johnson	1666	600
36	John Jenkins	1666	1200
36	Richard Kellum	1666	850
37	Major John Tillney	1666	350
64	Col. John Stringer	1673	1050
80	Arthur Robins	1667	1000
80	Anne Tofft	1667	2600
81	John Goring	1667	1000
81	Henry Smith	1667	1000
81	Wm. White	1667	400
82	Wm. Hickman	1667	1000
83	Robert Hutchinson	1667	1250
83	John Wise	1668	1060
176	John Wise	1668	1060
176	Thos. Teakel	1668	350
186	Major John Tilney	1668	1000
186	Same	1668	1100
258	Thos. Leatherbury	1669	1400
258	Geo. Johnson	1669	950
259	Same	1669	400
259	Ann Toft	1669	2000
265	Mr. Wm. Custis	1669	300
266	Wm. Taylor	1669	1000
266	John Walter	1669	200
266	Teage Miskett	1669	300
267	Mr. Dan'l Foxcraft	1669	600
267	Thos. Gittinis	1669	450
267	Wm. Blake	1669	300
269	Henry Scott	1669	400
268	Martyn Moore	1669	400
268	Roger Trenon, assignee of John Orily	1669	300
268	Thos. Orily	1669	300

286	John Wallop alias Warlow	1670	3050
313	Wm. Brittingham	1670	450
316	Lt. Col. Wm. Kendall	1670	10,500
312	Same	1670	200
388	Daniel Jennifer and Anne, his wife, late Anne Toft	1672	11,300
388	Same	1672	5000
393	John Kendall	1672	700
401	Deborah Brown	1672	3600
403	John Rolles	1672	200
330	John Walter	1670	400
405	Devereaux Browne	1670	3700
413	John Kendall	1673	200
458	John Taylor	1673	34
475	Wm. Taylor	1673	1000
478	Charles Ratcliff	1673	1300
439	Ambrose White	1672	450
482	Wm. and Mary, son and dau. of Wm. Kendall	1672	6000
496	Wm. Blake	1672	300
497	Wm. Jerman	1672	300
498	Arthur Frame	1672	500
505	Charles Scarburgh	1673-4	4350
510	Col. Wm. Kendall	1674	268
514	John Wallop alias Waddilow	1674	450
514	Sam'l Taylor	1674	700
514	Edmund Boeman	1674	250
527	George Johnson	1674	1100
529	Lt. Col. Jno. Tillne	1674	1600
531	Ambrose White	1674	2000
533	Capt. John West, Chas. Scarburgh, Capt. Edmund Scarburgh, Mrs. Tabetha Browne	1674	8000
535	John Kendall	1674	400
540	Hugh Yeo	1674	2050
541	Mrs. Anne Beate	1674	1350
542	Major Edmund Boeman and Capt. Southey Littleton	1647	2264

HENRICO COUNTY

BOOK No. 8

70	Mathew Branch	1696	50
86	James Cock	1697	311
105	Capt. Francis Eps	1697	68
128	Giles Webb	1697	528
138	Capt. Thos. Cock	1698	49
139	Wm. Cock	1698	256
144	Wm. Burton	1698	144
159	Henry Randolph	1698	731A. 1R. 30po.
159	Joseph Royall	1698	235
160	Same	1698	50
160	Francis Epes	1698	60
161	Abraham Womacke	1698	200
167	Capt. Wm. Soan	1698	3150
168	John Puckett	1698	257
168	Thomas Pollard	1698	940
169	James Franklin	1698	426
172	Gideon Macon	1698	148
187	Robert Burton	1699	1300
191	John Pleasants	1699	3087
236	Same	1699	98
237	John Davis	1699	200
242	Mrs. Mary Ligon	1699	——
268	Richard Dearelove	1700	223
270	Wm. Randolph	1700	1230
273	Ephraim Garthright	1700	175
287	John Davis	1700	254A. 3R. 8po.
307	Robert Burton, Sr.	1701	300
318	John Bolling	1701	50
319	Francis Perce	1701	137
321	John Woodson, Sr.	1701	1020
322	John Pleasants	1701	2994A. 2R. 35per.
372	Benjamin Harrison	1701	3313
373	Thomas Cock	1701	628
390	Thomas Farrar	1701	126
399	John Worsham and Francis Patterson	1701	924
407	Wm. Traylor	1701	700
429	Robert Grigg	1702	400

628	John Granger 1704	72
628	John Gill 1704	235
629	Robert Woodson 1704	171
646	Robert Bolling 1705	50
648	Mary Ascough 1705	633
661	Wm. Hatcher, Sr. 1705	540
665	Charles Evans 1705	140
673	Allenson Clarke and Chas. Russell 1705	945
674	John Bolling, Edward Bowman and Jno. Bowman 1705	1146
679	Abraham Michaux 1705	574
688	Wm. Byrd 1705	385
696	Richard Holmes 1705	252
713	Robert Hudson and Thos. Pollard, Jr....1705	940
722	Richard Cock, Jr. 1706	570
731	Richard Bland 1706	5644
734	John Worsham, Jr. 1706	190
737	Chas. Evans ....1706 1468A. 1R. 28p.	
738	John Tullit 1705 17,650	

BOOK No. 10

42	Abraham Salle 1711	232
73	Tarlton Woodson 1713	102
74	Charles Evans 1713	200
82	Wm. Shepard and Richard Baker 1713	400
93	Joseph Pleasants 1713	1029
94	John Pleasants 1713	1385
123	Abraham Michaux 1713	850
125	John Calvet 1714	100
128	David Pattison 1714	400
130	Henry Gill 1714	500
132	Wm. Lead 1714	500
132	Charles Hudson and John Bradley 1714	608
132	Charles Fleming 1714	1427
133	Peter Dutoy 1714	400
134	John Burton 1714	341
139	James Christian 1714	382

142	Stephen Chastiene	1714	138
148	Wm. Clark, Sr.	1714	229
151	Charles Fleming	1714	732
156	Stephen Chasteane	1714	280
157	John Pleasants	1714	541
161	Charles Evans	1714	577
148	Thomas Christian	1714	400
162	Wm. Grills	1714	400
163	Charles Fleming	1714	670
166	John Woodson and Charles Fleming....	1714	1278
167	Anthony Rappeene	1714	190
171	Amos Ladd	1714	1085
177	Richard Grills	1714	3000
190	Wm. Cox	1714	440
191	Thomas Harrod	1714	448
193	John Perkinson	1714	150
210	John Elles	1714	500
210	Gilly Grimurrin	1714	292
210	Gilly Grimurren	1714	500
216	Ebenezer Adams	1714	670
216	Robt. Woodson, Jr.	1714	1494
217	Thomas Mims	1714	500
217	Richard Cocke	1714	2497
217	John Farlar, Jr.	1714	300
217	John Steavens	1714	125
229	Isaac Lafeit	1714	133
235	Maj. John Bolling	1714	1388
237	John Woodson	1715	1596
237	Same	1715	348
238	John Pleasants	1715	258
238	John Woodson	1715	892
239	John Pleasants	1715	1309
240	Wm. Womack	1715	950
241	Thomas Bayley	1715	350
244	Thomas Watkins	1715	400
245	Bartholomew Staval	1715	318
246	Charles Christian	1715	400

321	Henry Anderson	1717	500
321	Majr. John Bolling	1717	300
321	Tarlton Woodson	1717	2307
324	John Bolling, Edward Bowman and John Bowman	1717	479
328	Henry Wilson	1717	500
329	Dorothy Pleasants	1717	463
329	Francis Sassin	1717	104
345	Micael Johnson	1717	500
345	Colo. Francis Epes	1717	1000
346	Francis Epes, Jr.	1717	285
346	Wm. Kennon	1717	42
347	Joseph Royall	1717	900
347	Amos Lead	1717	472
347	Godfrey Fouler and George Archer	1717	500
364	Bartholomew Dupee	1717	133
364	Anthony Trebue	1717	522
365	Stephen Sunter	1717	400
369	James Branch	1717	31
377	Ralph Hudspith	1718	370
377	Samuel Garthrite	1718	143
377	James Legran	1718	365
378	James Aken, Sr.	1718	340
378	Charles Fleming	1718	1430
378	Thomas Jefferson and others	1718	1500
379	James Moss	1718	400
379	John Barnes, Jr. and Wm. Barnes	1718	365
380	James Johnson	1718	400
380	John Johnson	1718	400
380	Owen Eaven	1718	150
381	Amos Lad	1718	250
381	Wm. Kernon	1718	1100
393	Henry Soane	1718	690
393	John Bolling	1718	800
392	Wm. Kennon	1718	900
409	Matthew Ligon and Richard Ligon, Jr.	1718	290
408	George Freeman	1718	400

89	Thomas Randolph	1722	670
91	Same	1722	1000
107	Daniel Croom	1722	400
108	Thomas Wilson	1722	59
108	John Jones	1722	52
109	Benjamin Watkins	1722	500
110	Benjamin Woodson	1722	178
110	David Pattison	1722	337
111	Anthony Rapeen	1722	400
157	John Gun	1722	250
158	Edward Scott	1722	400
158	Robert Blaws, Joseph Woodson, John Woodson and John Woodson, Jr.	1722	400

YORK COUNTY.

Book No. 7.

Page	Name	Date	No. acres
25	Wm. Whittacar	1680	400
46	Robert Everett	1680	280
47	Thomas Cheesman	1680	550
61	John Wright	1680	84
122	Edward Harwood and Thomas Platt	1682	759
123	Argoll Blackstone	1682	389
138	Samuel Signell	1682	455
178	John Smith	1682	78
217	Tho. Wotton and Henry Haywood	1682	178
280	John Page	1683	330
292	Peter Glenister	1683	80
314	David Condon	1683	114
336	Wm. Cole	1683	618
353	Robert Read	1684	350
360	Joseph Firth	1684	150
382	Richard Palmer	1684	223
397	John Wright and Thomas Carroll	1684	102

BOOK No. 9.

135	James Whaley	1698	200
130	Edmd. Jenings	1698	694
137	Daniel Park	1698	30
137	Same	1698	100
158	Joseph White	1698	50
201	Robt. Shields and John Doswell	1699	73
204	John Doswell	1699	294
212	Samuel Toplady	1699	202
223	Thomas Harwood	1699	202
293	Miles Cary	1700	256
347	Wm. Huitt	1701	150
517	Arthur Lunn	1703	50
570	John Tullet	1703	391
592	Wm. Pattison	1704	300
643	Stephen Fousce	1704	23
608	Edward Thomas	1705	220

BOOK No. 10.

1	John Adduston Rogers	1710	270
6	Philip Dunford	1711	11
6	Wm. Moss	1711	27½
39	Wm. Sheldon	1711	150
43	Francis Callohill and Giles Tavenor	1711	48
54	John Northen	1711	100
71	Francis Tyler	1713	38
77	Henry Hayward	1713	48½
124	Wm. Row	1714	174½
125	Elizabeth Chermeson	1714	100
171	Jonathan Dewitt	1714	100
218	John Drewry	1714	15
219	Giles Tavernor	1714	13A. 34chs.
418	Joseph Walker	1719	162

BOOK No. 11.

51	John Custis	1720	50
141	Jonathan Drewitt	1722	47A. & 1½

236 George Walker 1723   183
343 John Brookes 1724   ½A.

BOOK No. 12.

326 John Hubbard 1725   21
340 Mrs. Mary Whaley 1725   16½

BOOK No. 13.

333 John Davis 1728   40
509 Robert Shield 1730   265
531 Lewis Davis 1730   26

BOOK No. 14.

323 Thomas Couser 1731   83

BOOK No. 15.

194 Thomas Roberts 1734   7
195   Same 1734   12½
206 Richard Pate 1734   40 ft. sq. of land

BOOK No. 23.

748 James Gemmill 1744   6½

BOOK No. 24.

535 Edward Peter 1746   127

BOOK No. 26.

57 Wm. Moss ....1747 24A. 4chs.

BOOK No. 28.

159 Robert Roberts 1747   81

BOOK No. 31.

631 Thomas Roberts 1755   44

BOOK No. 32.

505 Benjamin Powell 1755   2 lotts or 1acre.
599 Landon Carter 1755   36½

Book No. 33.

435	Robert Smith	1758	115
567	Simpkin Bryan	1759	77
887	Samuel Roberts	1760	34½

Book No. 35.

317	John Blair	1763	½

Book No. 38.

807	John Robinson	1769	26

Book No. 40.

783	John Tazewell	1772	3 lots

COMMONWEALTH'S GRANTS OR PATENTS.

629	Wm. Nelson	1790	63½
629	Same	1790	48¾
630	Same	1790	255

SUSSEX COUNTY.

Book No. 35.

Page	Name	Date	No. acres
302	Joshua Hartshorn	1763	18
312	Nicholas Massenburg	1763	62
399	Henry Gee	1763	123
408	Charles Judkins	1763	250
417	Thomas Myers	1763	254
418	John Stokes	1763	54
543	Wm. Blunt	1764	26

Book No. 36.

559	John Mason, Jr.	1764	68½
594	Geo. Long	1764	920

619 Thos. Goodwynne 1764   100
641 Henry Moss 1764   23
670 Howell Briggs 1764   4012
695 Benj. Wyche 1764   200
714 Nathl. Peeples 1765   230
847 Bartholomew Betts 1765   104
941 Thomas King 1766   241
1077 Wm. Rogers, Jr. 1766   133

BOOK No. 37.

24 Richard Pepper 1767   264
235 James Bell 1768   117

BOOK No. 38.

76 David Blanks 1769   20
828 Richard Stewart 1769   395

BOOK No. 39.

124 Thomas Griffin 1770   179
178 John Bell, Jr. 1770   110
285 Stith Parham 1771   344
450 James Stewart 1771   75

BOOK No. 40.

490 James Chappell 1771   370
605 John Lamb 1771   30
652 John Fort 1772   41
793 Wm. Connelly 1772   210
871 Richd. Avery 1772   101
874 Henry Briggs 1772   65
881 Peter Cain 1772   244

BOOK No. 41.

29 Benjamin Rogers 1772   45
38 Hollom Sturdivant 1772   35
111 Pettway Johnson 1773   1780
164 Michael Blow 1773   400

165	Thomas Fisher	1773	113½
334	Josiah Freeman	1773	50
341	Ambrose Grizzard	1773	575
364	Faddy Jarrad	1773	701
375	Joseph Lane	1773	79

Book C.

525	John Jones	1781	46
553	David Jones	1781	240

Book E.

19	Thomas Lewellin	1775	62
855	Thomas Avent	1780	19

Book H.

479	Thomas Avant	1783	80
483	Barham Moore	1783	60
497	John Bonner	1783	45
500	John Kelley	1783	50
502	Littlebury Mason	1783	80
543	Same	1783	87½
554	Michael Malone	1783	5¾
512	Joshua Thorp	1783	37½

Book M.

486	Jesse Hargrave	1784	102

Book N.

1	John Powell	1784	137
262	Wm. Nicholson	1784	109½
502	Capt. Judkins Hunt	1784	26

Book O.

549	John Saunders	1785	33½

Book Q.

320	Isaac Bendall	1785	20¾

Book R.

| 566 | Wm. Cocke, Jr. | 1785 | 39 |
| 624 | John Johnson | 1785 | 86 |

Book S.

291	John Smith	1785	51
506	Nathl. Robinson	1785	79
519	Judkins Hunt	1785	29½

Book V.

| 542 | Cyreel Avery | 1785 | 1234½ |
| 546 | Howell Jones | 1785 | 622 |

Book X.

31	Thos. Creagh	1785	150
357	Jones Glover	1785	312
666	Col. Charles Williams	1785	100

Book No. 6.

| 453 | Wm. Andrews | 1786 | 254½ |

Book No. 8.

237	Jesse Hargrave	1787	30
238	Henry Cook	1787	683½
463	Lawrence House	1787	218

Book No. 12.

| 278 | Richard Harwell | 1787 | 233½ |

Book No. 13.

| 617 | Wood Heath | 1787 | 236½ |

Book No. 14.

| 37 | Wm. Birdsong | 1787 | 253½ |
| 39 | Wm. Chappell | 1787 | 263 |

Book No. 16.

133 Nathl. Land 1787   200

Book No. 17.

165 John Masserburg 1788   47¼
547 Benj. Owens 1788   18

Book No. 18.

489 James Robinson 1788   395½

Book No. 19.

74 Wm. Mason 1788   30
604 Charles Judkins 1789   10

Book No. 23.

493 John Judkins 1791   131

Book No. 24.

64 Michael Molone 1791   78½

Book No. 25.

47 Nathl. Wyche 1791   740
316 John Judkins 1791   68

Book No. 32.

31 Peter Jennins 1794   26¼

Book No. 33.

278 Thomas Mason 1795   12¾
279 Thomas Mason 1795   15

Book No. 36.

581 Benj. Johnson 1797   10
592 Benj. Thomas 1797   10½

Book No. 37.

431 Thos. Hicks 1797   7½
433 Hermon Horn 1797   348½

BOOK No. 39.

432	Gray Gilliam	1797	20
637	Jesse Zills	1797	10¼

BOOK No. 40.

276	Robert Linn	1798	25

PATRICK COUNTY.

Page	Name	Date	No. acres

BOOK No. 28.

519	James Harris	1793	85

BOOK No. 31.

171	Edward Pedigo	1794	31
246	George Hairston	1795	150
363	John Hook	1795	1190
378	Same	1795	394
595	Geo. Hairston	1795	729

BOOK No. 32.

173	David Lawson	1795	598
495	James Lyon, Sr.	1795	97
495	Same	1795	118
565	Joseph Gallego and John Augustus Chevallie	1796	8000
619	Benj. Chambers	1796	40,194½

BOOK No. 33.

249	John Hall	1795	261
377	James Lyon, Sr.	1795	23
424	John A. Chevallie and Joseph Gallego	1796	32,000
457	Jedediah Leeds	1796	24,265
577	Miller Easley	1796	122

Book No. 34.

20	James Ternain	1796	45,000
332	Adam Turner	1796	73
333	Jacob Adams	1796	165
333	John Burnett	1796	39
388	Wm. Bowyer and Wm. Breckenridge...	1796	65,000
392	James Potiet, Jr.	1796	137
384	Thos. Southcomb	1796	14,000
517	Joseph Reynolds	1796	209
518	Wm. Deal	1796	55
523	Augustine Thomas	1796	47
569	Jno. Armstrong	1796	4,400
694	Wm. Coleman and Horatio Gates Haveland	1796	25,000
644	Clement Rogers	1796	55
644	John Tompson	1796	58
645	Moses Reynolds	1796	57
646	Laurence Lee	1796	316
646	John Dillian	1796	40
143	Hugh Woods and Robt. Stockton	1796	200

Book No. 35.

22	John Barclay	1796	35,123
25	Same	1796	24,090½
61	Wm. Thorp	1796	101
128	David Robertson	1796	422
152	Joseph Reynolds	1796	18
164	Same	1796	150
169	Same	1796	312

Book No. 36.

34	Wm. Bowyer and Wm. Breckenridge..	1796	35,000
117	Jas. Perkins, Saml. Blagge, Gardiner L. Chandler and Wm. Coleman	1796	14,700
302	Henry Lee	1796	70,000
407	Blizard Magruder	1796	1843
484	Rodham Moore	1797	21

484 Bartemus Reynolds 1797 232
486 Michael Ahart 1797 147
488 Wm. Williams 1797 22
506 John Ogle 1797 79
539 Joshua Haynes 1797 93
543 John Hook 1797 3023
543 Same 1797 100
545 Same 1797 124
546 Same 1797 231

BOOK No. 37.

57 Owen Ruble 1796 669
342 Elihu Ayre 1797 170
346 Francis Turner and Robt. Rowan 1797 1223
356 Geo. Carter 1797 145
370 Tedrick Ewes 1797 86
396 Wm. Fuson 1797 41
397 Benj. Garrott 1797 142
398 Joshua Haynes 1797 71
400 John Hook 1797 13,402
532 Levi Jones 1797 222
582 Thomas Dodson 1798 47
585 Jonathan Shipman and Asher Waterman 1798 700

BOOK No. 38.

1 Benj. Haskill 1797 25,000
72 Jas. Perkins, Saml. Blagge, Gardiner L.
   Chandler and Wm. Coleman 1797 12,095
229 Wm. Armstrong 1798 120
248 Geo. Hairston 1798 30
248 Same 1798 104
249 Same 1798 143
254 Same 1798 228
263 Same 1798 30
267 Same 1798 133
268 Wm. Armstrong 1798 50
268 Same 1798 55
272 Jonathan Shipman and Asher Waterman 1798 2000
314 Beverly Spencer 1798 150

GOOCHLAND COUNTY.

95	Chas. Hudson	1733	1060
96	Henry Wood	1733	1600
99	Saml. Nuckols	1733	675
99	Richd. Randolph	1733	4150
101	Wm. Moseley	1733	400
102	Same	1733	200
103	John Jones	1733	400
104	Leonard Ballow	1733	340
105	John Phillips	1733	400
106	James Daniel	1733	330
106	John Stoval	1733	200
107	Leonard Ballow	1733	400
107	Geo. Freeman	1733	400
111	Ebenezer Adams	1733	1150
113	Barth. Stoval	1733	250
119	John Johnson	1733	400
121	Joseph Fuqua	1733	350
121	John Maddox	1733	400
124	Robt. Adams	1733	400
130	Wm. Bradshaw	1733	390
133	Thos. Carter	1733	400
134	Hugh Morris	1733	400
135	John Stoval	1733	400
137	Robert Adams	1733	400
139	Wm. Taber	1733	88
141	Noel Burton	1733	400
146	John Pleasant	1733	400
149	Wm. Randolph	1733	3800
160	Andrew Crew	1733	200
168	Lewis Jenkins	1733	250
169	Jas. Terrel	1733	400
174	John Price	1733	400
174	Thos. Baugh	1733	400
178	John Lewis	1733	150
179	John Price	1733	400
180	Richd. Ward	1733	450
182	Richd. Williamson	1733	400

183	Jas. Terrell	1733	400
188	John Williams	1733	400
193	John Key	1734	400
194	Same	1734	145
195	Chas. Lynch	1734	291
149	John Sowell	1734	100
149	Edmund Wood	1734	400
200	Henry Wood	1734	200
207	Jas. Defaux	1734	130
208	Henry Hatcher	1734	400
210	Joseph Smith	1734	287
211	Wm. Holladay	1734	400
214	Thos. Ballow	1734	150
220	John Hawkins	1734	400
221	Joseph Smith, Edwin Hickman and Jonathan Clarke	1734	3277
225	Merry Webb	1734	200
227	John Cobbs	1734	400
232	John Godley	1734	400
234	James Terry	1734	400
241	Chas. Toney	1734	400
242	Same	1734	400
243	Thos. Edwards	1734	200
248	Thos. Harbour	1734	400
255	Wm. Arrington	1734	400
257	John Cobbs	1734	400
271	John Parish	1734	400
271	Thos. Murrell	1734	71
272	Henry Cary	1734	320
272	Arthur Hopkins	1734	2000
284	Wm. Mayo	1734	3000
285	John Nash	1734	400
296	Wm. Verdeman	1734	200
297	Arthur Osborne	1734	400
302	Robert Lewis	1734	174
303	Abraham Venables	1734	780
304	Thomas Sowell	1734	550

345	John Crawford	1734	190
346	John Kent	1734	500
346	Wm. Sanders	1734	400
347	Benj. Wheeler	1734	300
348	James Defur	1734	150
348	Wm. Matlock	1734	190
349	John Crawford	1734	400
350	Benj. Wheeler	1734	300
354	Humphrey Parish	1734	400
356	Joel Terrell and David Lewis	1734	2300
358	Arthur Hopkins	1734	200
360	Josias Payne	1734	154
365	Jonas Lawson	1734	200
370	Nicholas Meriwether	1734	220
372	John Nash	1734	400
383	Christopher Cawthorn	1734	400
385	Geo. Payne, Jr.	1734	190
388	Same	1734	400
396	Jno. Cunningham	1734	200
404	Christopher Cawthorn	1734	250
413	George Hilton	1734	332
417	Welcome W. Hodges	1734	400

CAROLINE COUNTY.

Page	Name	Date	No. acres

Book No. 13.

276	John Cheadle and Thos. Hackett	Sep. 2, 1728	400
388	John Sutton	Sep. 2, 1728	175
323	Robert Holmes	Sep. 28, 1728	317
400	Edward Yarborough	Sep. 27, 1729	200
400	Daniel and Henry White	Sep. 27, 1729	500
400	Isaac Allen	Sep. 27, 1729	50
415	John Partle	Sep. 27, 1730	200
445	Henry Raines	June 2, 1730	250

445	Same	June 2, 1730	436
488	Thos. Ham, Sr.	Sep. 28, 1730	580
489	Micajah Chiles	Sep. 28, 1730	379
489	John Clarke	Sep. 28, 1730	207
490	Thomas Carr	Sep. 28, 1730	570
490	John Harris	Sep. 28, 1730	162
491	Richard and Francis Fowler	Sep. 28, 1730	137½

BOOK No. 14.

151	Robert Beverley	Feb. 24, 1730	4254
159	Robert Chandler	June 26, 1731	357
162	John Ellis	June 26, 1731	530
286	Wm. Marshall	Aug. 25, 1731	150
287	Zachariah Martin	Aug. 25, 1731	306
373	John Sandland	Jan. 25, 1731	400
400	Richard Mauldin	April 11, 1732	387
432	Thomas Carr	April 11, 1732	2530
457	Thomas Carr	July 1, 1732	400
512	Thos. Catlett	Sep. 28, 1732	66
529	Robert Beverley	Sep. 28, 1732	929
445	Henry Raines	June 2, 1730	436

BOOK No. 15.

50	Wm. Bell	June 20, 1733	162
66	John Sutton	June 20, 1733	400
76	Lewis Burwell	June 20, 1733	400
82	Charles Gooddal	June 20, 1733	915
126	Wm. Beverley	Oct. 26, 1733	4254
176	Thomas Catlett	Mar. 23, 1733	1376
286	Richard Long	Aug. 20, 1734	1165

BOOK No. 16.

| 144 | Benj. Walker | Aug. 9, 1735 | 200 |
| 490 | George Wilson and John Clark | Jan. 10, 1735 | 277 |

BOOK No. 17.

| 18 | George Woodroof | Mar. 15, 1735 | 400 |
| 421 | Hugh Rea | Oct. 3, 1737 | 118 |

Book No. 18.

34	Robert Baber	July 20, 1738	10
36	Samuel Coleman	July 20, 1738	100

Book No. 19.

714	Thomas Collins	Aug. 20, 1740	90
814	Joseph Berry	Dec. 1, 1740	286

Book No. 20.

25	Wm. Crutchfield	Oct. 15, 1741	596
430	Wm. Pemberton and Easter Bell	July 30, 1742	83
480	Wm. Trigg	Mar. 30, 1743	157

Book No. 21.

518	William Stayton	Aug. 30, 1743	167
520	Henry Bartlett	Aug. 30, 1743	68

Book No. 22.

199	Wm. Woodford	Aug. 30, 1744	36

Book No. 24.

169	Wm. Beverley	Mar. 5, 1745	70

Book No. 28.

357	Laurence Taliaferro	Jan. 12, 1747	162

Book No. 31.

201	Richard Davenport	Sep. 15, 1752	396
503	William Burdett	July 10, 1755	81½

Book No. 32.

405	Wm. Daniel, Jr.	Oct. 17, 1754	1000

Book No. 33.

475	Edmund Pendleton	Aug. 19, 1758	96
936	Henry Terrell	Sep. 26, 1760	379

BOOK No. 34.

335	William Lindsey	Aug. 10, 1759	294
806	John Sutton	Feb. 14, 1761	400
936	Duncan Graham	Aug. 7, 1761	72
1033	James Murry	July 12, 1762	95
1035	Wm. Boutwell	July 12, 1762	18

BOOK No. 35.

461	Laurence Taliaferro	Aug. 30, 1763	12

BOOK No. 36.

562	Wm. Quarles	June 27, 1764	15
913	John Philips	Oct. 31, 1765	32
1056	Laurence Taliaferro	July 10, 1767	12

BOOK No. 37.

194	John Micou	Sep. 10, 1767	138
250	Laurence Battaile	July 20, 1768	20

BOOK No. 38.

489	Ignatius Raines	Oct. 24, 1768	47
524	John Chiles	Apr. 6, 1769	255

BOOK No. 39.

55	David Chivis	May 12, 1770	6½
180	George Turner	Aug. 27, 1770	63

BOOK No. 41.

450	Anthony Thornton, Jr.	June 15, 1773	65

COMMONWEALTH GRANTS AND PATENTS.

Page	Name	Date	No. acres
	BOOK D.		
325	John Minor	Dec. 11, 1780	200
326	John Pickett	Dec. 11, 1780	400
327	Mace Pickett	Dec. 11, 1780	339

Book E.

841 Robert Gilchrist ....Dec. 11, 1780   ½

Book No. 9.

673 John Hord ....July 18, 1787   53

Book No. 14.

391 James Miller ....Dec. 13, 1787   78

Book No. 15.

708 Thomas Lomax ....April 17, 1788   58
709 Thomas Lomax ....April 17, 1788   13
728 Robert Beverley ....April 17, 1788   114

Book No. 28.

624 William Petross ....July 26, 1793   18

VIRGINIA REVOLUTIONARY SOLDIERS

(Continued from Vol. VI.)

Dailey, James, Drummer, Contl. Line, 3 years' service.
Wallace, James, Private, State Line, 3 years' service.
Dunn, John, Private, Contl. Line, 3 years' service.
Brown, Robert, Trumpeter, Va. Cavalry, 3 years' service.
Bridgman, Franklin, Private, State Line, 3 years' service.
Madison, William, Private, State Line, 3 years' service.
Clark, William, Private, State Line, 3 years' service.
Crump, Thomas, Private, State Artillery, 3 years' service
Hill, John, Private, State Artillery, 3 years' service.
Zimmerman, William, Sgt., Contl. Line, 3 years' service.
Hix, Edward, Private, Contl. Line, 3 years' service.
Lowe, John, Private, Contl. Line, 3 years' service.
Lowe, Thomas, Sgt., Contl. Line, 3 years' service.
Cooper, Spencer, Corporal, Contl. Line, 3 years' service.
Owl, Robert, Private, Contl. Line, 3 years' service.
Bowers, Philip, Private, Contl. Line, 3 years' service.
Harris, Walter, Private, Contl. Line, 3 years' service.
Andrews, Jesse, Sgt., Contl. Line, 3 years' service.
Parker, Jeremiah, Sgt., Contl. Line, 3 years' service.
Cunningham, Nathaniel, Sgt., Contl. Line, 3 years' service.
Cannafax, Edward, Private, Contl. Line, 3 years' service.
Learwood, Josiah, Private, Contl. Line, 3 years' service.
Tucker, James, Sgt., Contl. Line, 3 years' service.
Ramble, Samuel, Private, Contl. Line, 3 years' service.
Perryman, Benone, Fifer, Contl. Line, 3 years' service.
Morgan, William, Private, Contl. Line, 7 years' service.
Baylis, William, Private, State Line, 3 years' service.
Moody, James, Captain, State Line, 3 years' service.
McSwain, Edward, Sgt., State Line, 3 years' service.
Deprist, Robert, Drummer, State Line, 3 years' service.
Angel, William, Private, State Line, 3 years' service.
Salmon, George, Sgt., Contl. Line, 3 years' service.
Branan, Thomas, Sgt., Contl. Line, 7 years' service.
Baytop, James, Captain, Contl. Line, 3 years 'service.
Baytop, John, Lieut., State Line, 3 years' service.

Stern, Charles, Sgt., Contl. Line, 3 years' service.
Waller, John, Sgt., Contl. Line, 3 years' service.
Dobbins, Charles, Private, Contl. Line, 3 years' service.
Stockley, Charles, Lieut., Contl. Line, 7 years' service.
Long, Reuben, Lieut., Contl. Line, 3 years' service.
Haley, William, Private, Contl. Line, 7 years' service.
White, William, Capt., decd., Contl. Line, 3 years' service;
warrant to John White Aug. 15, 1783.
Edwards, John, Private, State Line, 3 years' service.
Flournoy, Samuel, Sgt., Contl. Line, 3 years' service.
Rhoads, William, Private, Contl. Line, 3 years' service.
Marshall, David, Private, State Line, 3 years' service.
Cottorel, William, Midshipman, State Navy, 3 years' service.
Elder, Ephraim, Private, Contl. Line, 3 years' service.
Summerson, Gavin, Midshipman, State Navy, 3 years' service.
Harrison, Val, Captain, Contl. Line, 3 years 'service.
Williams, Henry, Private, Contl. Line, 3 years' service.
Flemister, Lewis, Private, Contl. Line, 7 years' service.
Ball, Aaron, Private, Contl. Line, 3 years' service.
Bridgman, Thomas, Private, Contl. Line, 3 years' service.
Bartley, William, Private, Contl. Line, 3 years' service.
Davis, John, Private, Contl. Line, 3 years' service.
Roe, John, Private, Contl. Line, 3 years' service.
League, James, Private, Contl. Line, 3 years' service.
Grymes, George, Sgt., Contl. Line, 3 years' service.
Gary, John, Sgt., Contl. Line, 3 years' service.
Roberts, John, Private, State Line, 3 years' service.
Nichols, John, Private, Contl. Line, 3 years' service.
Suart, James, Private, Contl. Line, 3 years' service.
Bransford, William, Private, Contl. Line, 3 years' service.
Boils, David, Private, Contl. Line, 3 years' service.
Fisher, Thomas, Private, Contl. Line, 3 years' service.
Hunt, William, Private, Contl. Line, 3 years' service.
Purcell, John, Private, Contl. Line, 3 years' service.
Branam, John, Private, Contl. Line, 3 years' service.
Green, John, Private, Contl. Line, 3 years' service.
Biglie, William, Private, Contl. Line, 3 years' service.
Taylor, Arch., Private, Contl. Line, 3 years' service.

Lee, James, Private, State Line, 3 years' service.
Hatton, William, Private, Contl. Line, 3 years' service.
Fletcher, Stephen, Private, Contl. Line, 3 years' service.
Woodford, Wm., Brig.-Gen., decd., Contl. Line, 3 years' service; John Woodford, heir, Aug. 20, 1783.
Burk, William, Private, Contl. Line, 3 years' service.
Haynes, William, Private, Contl. Line, 3 years' service.
Jones, Richard, Sgt., Contl. Line, 3 years' service.
Barnett, Ambrose, Private, Contl. Line, 3 years' service.
O'Neal, Farrell, Sgt., Contl. Line, 3 years' service.
Buck, John, Private, State Line, 3 years' service.
Roberts, Obedience, Private, Contl. Line, 3 years' service.
Clift, William, Private, Contl. Line, 3 years' service.
Arnold, John, Sgt., Contl. Line, 3 years' service.
Mulin, Anthony, Private, Contl. Line, 3 years' service.
Perry, John, Cornet, Contl. Line, 3 years' service.
Brown, John, Private, Contl. Line, 3 years' service.
Monro, George, Dr., Surgeon, Contl. Line, 3 years' service.
Brady, Luke, Private, Contl. Line, 3 years' service.
McCormack, Adam, Private, Contl. Line, 3 years' service.
Camble, Dennis, Private, Contl. Line, 3 years' service.
Miller, Javan, Lieut., Contl. Line, 7 years' service.
Richeson, Walker, Lieut., Contl. Artillery, 3 years' service.
Wood, James, Private, Contl. Line, 3 years' service.
Ogden, Matthew, Private, Contl. Line, 3 years' service.
Conway, Joseph, Lieut., Contl. Line, 7 years' service.
Smithers, Stephen, Sgt., Contl. Line, 7 years' service.
Biggs, John, Private, Contl. Line, 3 years' service.
Tapley, Thomas, Private, Contl. Line, 3 years' service.
Curl, Richard, Private, Contl. Line, 3 years' service.
Ross, Val., Private, Contl. Line, 3 years' service.
Wood, Nicholas, Private, Contl. Line, 3 years' service.
Tinsley, Jonathan, Private, Contl. Line, 3 years' service.
Scott, John, Private, Contl. Line, 3 years' service.
Kirkpatrick, James, Private, Contl. Line, 3 years' service.
Thayar, William, Sgt.-Major, Contl. Line, 3 years' service.
Wood, William, Corporal, Contl. Line, 3 years' service.
Plummer, Armistead, Private, Contl. Line, 3 years' service.

Ransone, Robert, Private, Contl. Line, 3 years' service.
Doyle, Robert, Private, Contl. Line, 3 years' service.
Price, David, Sgt., Contl. Line, 3 years' service.
Hopkinstock, Charles, Private, Contl. Line, 3 years' service.
Bunn, David, Private, Contl. Line, 3 years' service.
Hill, Thomas, Private, Contl. Line, 3 years' service.
McNamara, Timothy, Private, Contl. Line, 3 years' service.
Hiliard, Joseph, Private, Contl. Line, 3 years' service.
Smith, James, Private, Contl. Line, 3 years' service.
Armstrong, Tobias, Private, Contl. Line, 3 years' service.
Fleming, William, Corporal, Contl. Line, 3 years' service.
Burk, John, Fifer, Contl. Line, 3 years' service.
Bowyer, Henry, Lieut., Contl. Line, 3 years' service.
Brekenridge, Robert, Lieut., Contl. Line, 7 years' service.
Payne, Joseph, Lieut., Contl. Line, 3 years' service.
Dener, Jacob, Sgt., Contl. Line, 3 years' service.
Pearman, Harrison, Private, Contl. Line, 3 years' service.
Fortune, Nathan, Private, Contl. Line, 3 years' service.
Carney, Patrick, Private, Contl. Line, 3 years' service.
Cox, William, Private, Contl. Line, 3 years' service.
Grissell, John, Private, Contl. Line, 3 years' service.
Merritt, Samuel, Private, Contl. Line, 3 years' service.
Hynes, James, Private, Contl. Line, 3 years' service.
Hart, Robert, Drum Major, Contl. Line, 3 years' service.
Bradley, John, Sgt., decd., Contl. Line, 3 years' service; Mary
    Bradley heir-at-law, Aug. 25, 1783.
Deiner, Jacob, Sgt., Contl. Line, 3 years' service.
Hart, Robert, Drum Major, Contl. Line, 3 years' service.
Lawless, Austin, Private, Contl. Line, 3 years' service.
Robertson, James, Lieut., decd., State Line, 3 years' service;
    Philip Barbour heir-at-law, Aug. 26, 1783.
Moore, Ralph, Corporal, Contl. Line, 3 years' service.
Steel, Wm., Lieut., State Navy, 3 years' service.
Boyling, Matthew, Drummer, Contl. Line, 3 years' service.
Emanuel, Henry, Private, Contl. Line, 3 years' service.
Monk, Joseph, Sgt., Contl. Line, 3 years' service.
Winston, William, Lieut., Contl. Line, 3 years' service.
Holmes, Lewis, Private, Contl. Line, 3 years' service.

Woolfolk, Francis, Sgt., Contl. Line, 3 years' service.
Jones, John, Private, Contl. Line, 3 years' service.
Altop, Thomas, Private, Contl. Line, 3 years' service.
Bailey, Edward, Sgt., decd., State Line, 3 years' service; William Newby Baily heir-at-law, Aug. 28, 1783.
Carter, John, Sailor, State Navy, 3 years' service.
Winphrey, John, Private, Contl. Line, 3 years' service.
Andrews, Benjamin, Sgt., State Line, 3 years' service.
Dickson, James, Private, State Line, 3 years' service.
Powell, Chas., Sgt., Contl. Line, 3 years' service.
Dennis, Henry, Private, Contl. Line, 7 years' service.
Simpson, John, Private, Contl. Line, 3 years' service.
Murray, Ralph, Private, Contl. Line, 3 years' service.
Chevalier, Anthony, Private, Contl. Line, 3 years' service.
Ward, George, Private, Contl. Line, 3 years' service.
Higgins, Robert, Captain, Contl. Line, 3 years' service.
Broom, John, Sgt., Contl. Line, 3 years' service.
Marks, Isaiah, Captain, Contl. Line, 3 years' service.
Copland, William, Corporal, Contl. Line, 3 years' service.
Auber, Peter, Private, decd., Contl. Line, 3 years' service; Wm. Vause heir-at-law, Aug. 30, 1783.
Beavers, John, Drummer, decd., State Line, 3 years' service; John Beavers, heir-at-law, Aug. 30, 1783.
Plummer, William, Sgt., Contl. Line, 3 years' service.
Beavers, Benjamin, Sgt., State Line, 3 years' service.
Flatford, Robert, Sgt., State Line, 3 years' service.
Galbreath, Robert, Sgt., Contl. Line, 3 years' service.
Gregory, William, Private, decd., Contl. Line, 3 years' service; Walter Gregory, heir-at-law, Sept. 1, 1783.
Gregory, Charles, Sgt., Contl. Line, 3 years' service.
Bonner, Richard, Sgt., Contl. Line, 3 years' service.
Jones, Peter, Corporal, Contl. Line, 3 years' service.
Rutter, Adam, Private, Contl. Line, 3 years' service.
Nuttall, Iverson, Midshipman, State Navy, 3 years' service.
Hewell, Thomas, Private, State Line, 3 years' service.
Puryear, Jesse, Private, Contl. Line, 3 years' service.
Cayner, Matt., Private, Contl. Line, 3 years' service.
Anderton, John, Private, State Line, 3 years' service.

Anderton, Isaac, Private, State Line, 3 years' service.
Stacey, John, Private, State Line, 3 years' service.
St. Leger, William, Private, State Line, 3 years' service.
Nicking, James, Sailor, State Navy, 3 years' service.
Sanders, Presley, Sgt., Contl. Line, 3 years' service.
Sanders, Joseph, Lieut., State Navy, 3 years' service.
Dydes, Robert, Seaman, State Navy, 3 years' service.
Nelms, Meredith, Seaman, State Navy, 3 years' service.
Winder, Jesse, Sgt., Contl. Line, 3 years 'service.
Shearman, Matt., Midshipman, State Navy, 3 years' service.
Hundley, Joshua, Private, Contl. Line, 3 years' service.
Melton, Hardy, Private, State Line, 3 years' service.
Griffin, Robert, Private, State Line, 3 years' service.
Packetts, Richard, State Line, 3 years' service.
Burk, Thomas, Private, Contl. Line, 3 years service.
Carroll, Berry, Private, State Line, 3 years' service.
Smith, John, Private, Contl. Line, 3 years' service.
Yarbrough, Charles, Lieut., Contl. Line, 3 years' service.
Farinholtz, David, Private, Contl. Line, 3 years' service.
Jones, Robert, Sgt., Contl. Line, 3 years' service.
Cavender, Joseph, Sgt., Contl. Line, 3 years' service.
Taylor, Richard, Lieut.-Col., Contl. Line, 3 years' service.
Newell, John, Sgt., Contl. Line, 3 years' service.
Shelton, David, Private, Contl. Line, 3 years' service.
Murphy, Michael, Private, Contl. Line, 3 years' service.
Hull, David, Private, Contl. Line, 3 years' service.
Bowling, Thornberry, Private, State Line, 3 years' service.
Hughes, James, Sgt., State Line, 3 years' service.
Gray, James, Sgt., Contl. Line, 3 years' service.
Penn, John, Sailor, State Navy, 3 years 'service.
Webb, Thomas, Private, State Line, 3 years' service.
Childress, Mosby, Private, Contl. Line, 3 years' service.
Morgan, Andrew, Sgt., State Line, 3 years' service.
Corbell, Peter, Corporal, State Line, 3 years' service.
Pope, Fortunatus, Sgt., State Line, 3 years' service.
Angell, William, Sailor, State Navy, 3 years' service.
Pullen, William, Sgt., State Line, 3 years' service.
Holmes, Isaac, Lieut., State Line, 3 years' service.

Woodson, Hughes, Captain, Contl. Line, 3 years' service.
Grigg, Lewis, Private, State Line, 3 years' service.
Grigg, Abner, Private, State Line, 3 years' service.
Huls, James, Private, Contl. Line, 3 years' service.
Bullen, Luke, Corporal, Contl. Line, 3 years' service.
Murray, Richard, Private, Contl. Line, 3 years' service.
Grant, Wm., Private, Contl. Line, 3 years' service.
Fleming, John, Sgt., State Line, 3 years' service.

NORTHAMPTON CO. MARRIAGE BONDS.

(Continued from Vol. VI., page 101)

June	25 1788.	William Bloxom and Keziah, widow of Charles Core.
Dec.	27, 1788.	Isaac Bratton and Nancy, dau. of Jacob Nottingham.
Feb.	17, 1789.	Doctor John Boisnard and Esther Robins, dau. of Edward Robins, decd.
Oct.	9, 1789.	John Blackwell and Margaret Jarvis, dau. of William.
Aug.	25, 1790.	James Barned and Sally Peck (or Pake), dau. of Elizabeth.
Feb.	12, 1790.	Anthony Burras and Mary Bell, widow of Robert Bell.
Aug.	3, 1790.	William Bloxom and Mary Johnson, widow of Robinson Johnson.
Sept.	14. 1790.	Edmund Bayly and Rachel Upham, dau. of John Upham, Snr.
Dec.	9, 1791.	Jonathan Bunting and Nancy White, dau. of Obedience White, decd.
July	4, 1791.	Daniel Benthall and Betsy Moore, dau. of Isaac Moore, decd.
May	21, 1791.	Jonas Belote and Susannah Holt, widow of Stewart Holt.
Nov.	26, 1792.	John Bird and Margaret ———. Elizabeth Parkinson her mother gives consent.

April	30, 1792.	John Booth and Esther Cowdry, dau. of William Cowdry.
July	31, 1793.	Kendall Belote and Sukey Widgen.
Dec.	20, 1793.	Laban Belote and Esther Dalby, dau. of John Dalby, Snr.
July	16, 1793.	William Bain and Susannah Dunton.
April	2, 1793.	Daniel Benthall and Elizabeth Nottingham.
May	2, 1793.	Nicholas Bloxom and Peggy Abel.
Jan.	16, 1794.	Arthur Bonnewell and Susanna Toleman.
June	13, 1794.	Henry Bingham and Ritta Collins.
Dec.	9, 1794.	Thomas Biggs and Ann Warren.
June	3, 1795.	Israel Bradford and Sally Waltham.
Feb.	11, 1795.	George Boggs and Margaret Stringer.
Dec.	19, 1795.	George Bell and Susey Bell.
March	24, 1796.	Nathaniel Benthall and Peggy O'Dear.
Sept.	13 1796.	James Biggs and Nice Courser.
Sept.	24, 1796.	Solomon Beavans and Esther Casey.
Dec.	15, 1796.	Azariah Benson and Sarah Cutler.
Jan.	31, 1797.	George Bradford and Elizabeth Boswell.
June	8, 1797.	William Bain and Betsy Robins.
July	10, 1797.	Holloway Bunting and Sally White.
Aug.	19, 1797.	Samuel Beavans and Molly Press.
Sept.	4, 1797.	William Bell, Jnr., and Esther Scott.
Oct.	26, 1797.	Abraham Becket and Sarah Thompson.
Nov.	18, 1797.	Thomas Bell and Tinney Chance, dau. of William Chance.
Dec.	20, 1797.	Nathaniel Bryan and Esther Mapp.
Aug.	30, 1798.	Doctor John Boisnard and Nancy Kendall.
July	31, 1798.	Hezekiah Beavans and Mary Morris.
May	30, 1798.	Thomas Bullock and Nancy Wingate.
May	22, 1798.	Ezekiel Badger and Mary Dunton.
May	24, 1798.	George Belote and Molly Wescoat.
Feb.	20, 1800.	John Burton and Ann Simkins.
Aug.	1, 1801.	Peter Bowdoin and Leah Teackle, dau. of Thomas Teackle.
June	8, 1801.	Jonathan Bool and Peggy Bool.
July	7, 1801.	Solomon Becket and Adah Liverpool.

June	24, 1717.	Thomas Custis of Accomac and Ann Kendall of Northampton.
Sept.	19, 1721	William Copeland and (woman's name not given).
Oct.	1, 1722.	Richard Carvey and Sarah Walter, widow.
May	25, 1723.	Thomas Cable and Sorrowful Margaret Kendall, widow.
Jan.	13, 1725.	Edward Carter and Mary Mapp.
March	3, 1732.	John Custis and Anne Kendall.
Feb.	21, 1733.	Jacob Costin and Sophia Savage.
May	17, 1736.	Simon Campbell and Joanna Roberts.
Dec.	30, 1747.	Michael Christian and Patience Michael, dau. of Joachim Michael.
Feb.	25, 1756.	Isaac Clegg and Peggy Major, dau. of William Major, Snr.
March	12, 1750.	Posthumous Core and Susannah Henderson.
Oct.	3, 1750.	Giles Cooke of Gloucester Co. and Margaret Savage, dau. of Esther Savage.
March	24, 1749.	Moses Cox of Norfolk Co. and Jeaca Mills, dau. of William Mills.
June	7, 1750.	William Christian and Keziah Blair, widow.
June	17, 1763.	Isaac Clegg and Esther Jacob.
May	8, 1764.	Isiah Clegg and Ann Belote, widow.
Aug.	29, 1763.	Henry Custis and Betty Downing, dau. of Arthur Downing.
April	15, 1758.	Charles Carpente and Elizabeth, dau. of John Custis Mathews.
June	15, 1758.	Savage Cowdry and Mary Barlow, dau. of the Rev. Henry Barlow.
Jan.	6, 1761.	William Christian and Matilda, dau. of Kelly and Beautifiler Johnson.
Dec.	15, 1760.	Edmund Core and Garris, dau. of Thomas Garris.
Dec.	7, 1764.	Francis Costin and Susannah Elliott, dau. of Thomas Elliott.
Jan.	12, 1768.	Charles Core and Betty Dalby.

Nov.	8, 1768.	Charles Carpenter and Bridget Matthews widow.
Nov.	11, 1769.	Thomas Cowdry and Sarah Jacob, dau. of Esau Jacob.
Feb.	20, 1770.	Michael Christian and Elizabeth Barlow.
March	8, 1768.	William Carey and Esther, dau. of John Custis Mathews.
March	23, 1773.	William Costin, son of Matthew, and Ann Trower, dau. of Robert Trower, decd.
Jan.	3, 1778.	Michael Conners and Margaret Griffith, widow.
Nov.	28, 1778.	Robert Cage and Esther Turner, dau. of John Fairbush Turner.
Nov.	20, 1779.	William Clegg and Susannah Dixon, dau. of John Dixon.
Dec.	21, 1779.	Nicholas Campbell and Anna Pigott, dau of Salem Pigott.
May	28, 1781.	William Carpenter and Tabitha Goffigon.
Feb.	14, 1782.	Henry Costin and Rachel Saunders, dau. of James Saunders, decd., and Tabitha his wife.
Jan.	8, 1782.	William Clay and Nancy Fitchett, dau. of Joshua Fitchett, decd.
Sept.	18, 1782.	Charles Carpenter and Susannah Waltham.
Dec.	16, 1783.	Obed Carey and Esther Nottingham.
Dec.	2. 1783.	Isaac Clegg and Agnes Piper, dau. of Josiah Piper, his dau. being 17 years old last April.
Jan.	15, 1783.	Eleazer Core and Keziah Rogers.
July	2, 1784.	Peter Clegg and Rosanna Milby.
Dec.	21, 1785.	Robert Clegg and Betsy Scott, widow of Wm. Scott.
Dec.	20, 1785.	John Core and Susannah Baker.
Dec.	13, 1785.	Samuel Costin and Elizabeth Griffith.
Nov.	25, 1786.	William Croswell and Elishe Stripe.
Dec.	14, 1786.	Hillary Clegg and Mary Ellegood.
Nov.	21, 1786.	John Collins and Ann Clegg.

Aug. 29, 1787.   Southey Cobb and Ann Pratt.
——— 1787.   William Caple and Ann Luke.
Aug. 14, 1787.   William Caple, son of Major Caple, and Esther O'Dear, dau. of William O'Dear.
March 23, 1787.   Thomas Clark and Elizabeth Warren.
March 1, 1787.   John Cowles and Rachel Stephens.

(To be continued)

ORANGE COUNTY MARRIAGE BONDS.

(Continued from Vol. VI., page 172)

Dec. 5, 1782.   Richard Gaines and Elizabeth Eastin. Consent of the mother, Elizabeth Eastin. Security—Philip Eastin.

Jan. 23, 1782.   James Goodale and Sally Harvey. Security—John Bell.

Dec. 31, 1782.   Isaac Hite, Jnr., and Nelly Madison. Security—A. Madison.

Nov. 11, 1782.   Charles Porter, Jnr., and Betsy Proctor. George Proctor, father, gives consent. Security—Benj. Hansford.

May 27, 1782.   Robert Rodes of Albemarle Co. and Liza Delaney. Security—And. Shepherd.

Nov. 27, 1782.   Achilles Stapp and Margaret Vawter. Mary Vawter, the mother, gives consent. Security—Richard White.

Dec. 21, 1782.   John Taylor and Mary Jarrell. John Jarrell, the father, gives consent. Security John Jarrell.

Sept. 25, 1782.   John Taylor and Elizabeth Kavenaugh. Security—John Price.

Nov. 11, 1782.   Richard Waugh and Elizabeth Brown. Security—And. Shepherd.

Sept. 10, 1782.   William White and Mary Brockman. Consent of Saml. Brockman, the father. Security—John Henderson, Jnr.

Dec. 12, 1783. John Ahart and Peggy Pearson, consent of father Robert Pearson. Security—Galen White.

Sept. 13, 1783. Reuben Bostin and Sarah Hawkins. Security—George Petty.

Jan. 14, 1783. Jacob Carrol and Tabitha Reynolds. Rachel Reynolds, the mother, gives consent. Security Benj. Griffy.

June 6, 1783. William Cave and Frances Christy. Consent of John Cave to son's, and Julius Christy to daughter's marriage. Security —Belfield Cave.

March 27, 1783. John Cootes and Sarah Thompson. Security—Edwd. Thompson.

March 10, 1783. Thomas Cox and Milly Oliver. Tabitha Oliver gives consent to daughter's marriage. Security—Joel Stodghill.

April 24, 1783. Thomas Davis and Elizabeth Early. Theodosia Early gives consent to daughter's marriage. Security—James Early.

June 19, 1783. Thomas Deering and Mary Raursey. Security—James Deering.

Feb. 24, 1783. William Fitzhugh and Ann Taliaferro. Lawrence Taliaferro, the father, consents. Security—Francis Dade.

Dec. 12, 1783. Joseph Ham and Sarah Hearen. Consent of parents, Francis and Sarah Hearen. Security—William Glass.

Dec. 30, 1783. John Hieatt and Sarah Arnold. Security— Michael Arnold.

Dec. 24, 1783. Lewis Hieatt and Barbary Allen. Security —Thomas Davis.

June 14, 1783. George Martin and Elizabeth Jones. Consent of father, Thos. Jones. Security— John Young.

Aug. 3, 1782. Micajah Neal and Milly Beasley. Consent of father, James Beasley. Security— Mace Pickett.

Dec. 11, 1783.   John Orant and Peggy Lintor. Security—
Ben. Hansford.

Dec. 22, 1783.   John Page, Jnr., with consent of parents
John Page, Snr., and Eliz. Page, to Mary
Collins, with consent of mother Mary
Collins. Security—William Alexander.

Sept. 8, 1783.   Ambrose Powell, with consent of father,
Thomas Powell, to Sally Britt, consent of
mother, Mary Britt. Security—James
Bush.

March 25, 1783.   Hezekiah Proctor and Nancy Young, with
consent of father, John Young. Security
—John Tunley.

May 22, 1783.   George Quisenberry and Jane Daniel. Security—Vivion Daniel.

March 27, 1783.   Richard Quinn and Ann Wood. Security
—Wm. Glass.

Dec. 25, 1783.   William Riddell, son of Lewis, and Joyce
Reddel. Security—John Godard.

May 1, 1783.   Thomas Davis of Spotsylvania and Susannah Hiatt. Security—John Hiatt.

June 2, 1783.   William Smith of Rockingham and Lucindy
Smith, dau. of Joseph Smith. Security—
Rice Smith.

June 19, 1783.   Charles Smith and Jane Morton. Consent
of father, Elijah Morton. Security—
Joseph Morton.

July 21, 1783.   John Straughan and Mary Sanders. Consent of father, Nathaniel Sanders. Se-
curity—James Sanders.

Feb. 11, 1783.   Reuben Taylor and Rebecca Moore. Security—James Taylor, Jr.

Aug. 24, 1783.   Vincent Vass and Elizabeth Manning,
widow. Security—Richard Dickinson.

Aug. 18, 1783.   Thomas Walker and Meseniah Powell, consent of mother, Mary Powell. Security—
Francis Powell.

July   8, 1783.   Wm. Crittenden Webb and Jane Buckner.
                    Security—W. Buckner.

Feb.   20, 1783.   Richard White and Catey Oliver, consent
                    of mother, Tabitha Oliver. Security—
                    Belfield Cave.

Nov.   5, 1783.   John Wright and Margaret Jones.

March 15, 1785.   William Alcock and Catey Bell. Security
                    —James Taylor.

Dec.   19, 1785.   Edwin Young and Frances Wright. Secur-
                    ity—Benjamin Hailey.

June   19, 1784.   William Vawter and Mary Rucker. Secur-
                    ity—James Stapp.

July   28, 1785.   Joel White and Frankey Rucker, dau. of
                    John Rucker. Security—Geo. Tomlin-
                    son.

July   20, 1785.   Johnson Watts and Sukey Davis, dau. of
                    George and Elizabeth Davis. Security—
                    James Taylor.

Jan.   13, 1785.   William Webb and Sarah Leathers, dau. of
                    John Leathers. Security—John Atkins.

Dec.   22, 1785.   Julian Watts and Mary Eve, dau. of Anne
                    Eve. Security—Prettyman Merry.

Nov.   24, 1785.   George Tomilson and Elizabeth White, dau.
                    of Henry White. Security—David (Dan-
                    iel ?) Cave.

Jan.   29, 1785.   James Tindar and Molly Shadrack, dau. of
                    Tobe Shadrack. Security—John Shad-
                    rack.

March 24, 1785.   John Smith and Elizabeth Warren. Secur-
                    ity—Thos. Bell.

April 13, 1785.   William Thompson and Acquilia Breeding.
                    Security—John Warren.

July   22, 1784.   Jesse Thornton and Ann Bohen, dau. of
                    Benj. and Ann Bohen. Security—George
                    Waugh.

Oct.   14, 1785.   Stephen Silvey and Frankey Dean. Secur-
                    ity—John Dean.
                    (To be continued)

REVOLUTIONARY PENSIONERS.

A census of pensioners for Revolutionary or military services with their names, ages and places of residence, as returned by the Marshals of the State of Virginia, under the Act for taking the Sixth Census, 1 June, 1840.

VIRGINIA—EASTERN DISTRICT.

Elkaneh Andrews, Accomac parish, Accomac Co., aged 77 years.

John Charnock, St. George's Parish, Accomac Co., aged 81 years.

Peter P. Copes, St. George's Parish, Accomac Co., aged 76 years.

William Kinnehan, St. George's Parish, Accomac Co., aged 91 years.

James Dunn, Fredericksville Parish, Albemarle Co., aged 80 years residing with James Dunn, Jnr.

James Gentry, Fredericksville Parish, Albemarle Co., aged 82 years.

William Harris, Snr., Fredericksville Parish, Albemarle Co., aged 80 years, residing with Wm. Harris, Jnr.

James Herring, Fredericksville Parish, Albemarle Co., aged 90 years.

George Gentry, Fredericksville Parish, Albemarle Co., aged 80 years, residing with James A. Johnson.

William Jordan, Fredericksville Parish, Albemarle Co., aged 79 years.

Adam Keblinger, Fredericksville Parish, Albemarle Co., aged 77 years.

Walter Watson, Fredericksville Parish, Albemarle Co., aged 79 years, residing with F. F. Kirby.

William Maupin, Fredericksville Parish, Albemarle Co., aged 80 years, residing with William Maupin, Jnr.

Richard Snow, Fredericksville Parish, Albemarle Co., aged 86 years.

John Wood, Snr., Fredericksville Parish, Albemarle Co., aged
    8; years.
Samuel Backsdale, St. Ann's Parish, Albemarle Co., aged 81
    years.
M. Bowen, St. Ann's Parish, Albemarle Co., aged 83 years,
    residing with William Bowen.
William Boyd, St. Ann's Parish, Albemarle Co., aged 90 years.
L. Drumheller, St. Ann's Parish, Albemarle Co., aged 75 years.
Richard Harrison, St. Ann's Parish, Albemarle Co., aged 83
    years.
John Jones, St. Ann's Parish, Albemarle Co., aged 82 years.
Jesse Lewis, St. Ann's Parish, Albemarle Co., aged 77 years.
William Morgan, St. Ann's Parish, Albemarle Co., aged 51
    years.
Thomas Burton, St. Ann's Parish, Albemarle Co., aged 83
    years, residing with William Reynolds.
David Strange, St. Ann's Parish, Albemarle Co., aged 78 years.
Larkin Foster, Amelia Co., aged 79 years.
Claiborn Wade, Amelia Co., aged 85 years.
Boswell Richards, Amelia Co., aged 53 years.
John Hutcherson, Amelia Co., aged 76 years.
Samuel Burton, Amelia Co., aged 85 years, residing with
    Charles F. Featherston.
Jones Gill, Amherst Co., aged 78 years.
William Lockard, Amherst Co., aged 110 years.
Thomas Coppedge, Amherst Co., aged 88 years, residing with
    Abraham Martin.
William Cashwell, Amherst Co., aged 78 years.
Alexander Logan, Amherst Co., aged 79 years.
James Evans, Amherst Co., aged 82 years, residing with Nancy
    Blair.
Jeremiah Brown, Amherst Co., aged 82 years.
Thomas Miles, Amherst Co., aged 79 years.
Dudley Calaway, Amherst Co., aged 90 years, residing with
    Susanna Thacker.
Jesse Beck, Amherst Co., aged 85 years.
Giles Davidson, Amherst Co., aged 78 years.
George Wise, Amherst Co., aged 83 years.

Ebenezer Hickok, Amherst Co., aged 81 years.

Jonathan Groomes, Bedford Co., aged 84 years, residing with Reuben Atkinson.

William Oliver, Bedford Co., aged 85 years, residing with James C. Oliver.

Thomas Andrews, Bedford Co., aged 79 years.

Thomas Pullin, Bedford Co., aged 78 years, residing with Joseph White.

John Arthur, Snr., Bedford Co., aged 82 years.

Isaac Gross, Snr., Bedford Co., aged 96 years.

Isaac Cundiff, Bedford Co., aged 79 years.

John McCormahay, Bedford Co., aged 78 years.

John Hudnall, Bedford Co., aged 78 years.

William J. Walker, Snr., Bedford Co., aged 79 years.

Francis Woods, Bedford Co., aged 79 years, residing with Wm. Green.

Jane Hancock, Bedford Co., aged 75 years, residing with Samuel Hancock.

John Buford, Bedford Co., aged 83 years.

John Carter, Bedford Co., aged 88 years, residing with Thos. Stewart.

William Arthur, Snr., Bedford Co., aged 78 years.

John Haynes, Bedford Co., aged 88 years, residing with Edmund Haynes.

Jonathan Dakin, Bedford Co., aged 79 years.

Henry Brown, Snr., Bedford Co., aged 79 years.

Abram Blankenship, Bedford Co., aged 82 years.

Gray Jones, Bedford Co., aged 84 years.

T. Minor, Snr., Bedford Co., aged 82 years.

John Wiggington, Bedford Co., aged 80 years.

Ann Hancock, Bedford Co., aged 79 years, residing with Mary Brown.

Jacob Shepperd, Bedford Co., aged 80 years.

David Saunders, Snr., Bedford Co., aged 80 years.

Joseph Crews, Bedford Co., aged 84 years.

John Halley, Bedford Co., aged 79 years.

Mary Beard, Bedford Co., aged 85 years.

William Davenport, Bedford Co., aged 75 years.

Richard Austin, Bedford Co., aged 84 years.

John Gills, Bedford Co., aged 80 years.

Ann Moseley, Bedford Co., aged 75 years.

Philip Lockhart, Bedford Co., aged 90 years.

Benjamin Robinson, Bedford Co., aged 85 years.

Jesse Vaughan, Brunswick Co., aged 83 years, residing with John M. Vaughan.

Ruel Lewis, Brunswick Co., aged 81 years.

Thomas Whitlock, Brunswick Co., aged 84 years.

William Wilkinson, Brunswick Co., aged 79 years.

Thomas Delbridge, Brunswick Co., aged 74 years.

William Starks, Buckingham Co., aged 85 years, residing with Wm. Harrison.

Abram Jones, Buckingham Co., aged 79 years.

John C. Harris, Buckingham Co., aged 85 years, residing with James Harris.

Mary Moseley, Buckingham Co., aged 75 years, residing with Rolfe Eldridge.

John Thomas, Buckingham Co., aged 80 years, residing with Gideon Howel.

John Harris, Buckingham Co., aged 79 years, residing with Joseph Riddle.

Timothy Scruggs, Buckingham Co., aged 86 years.

James Routon, Buckingham Co., aged 79 years.

Olive Branch, Buckingham Co., aged 80 years.

William Thornhill, Buckingham Co., aged 82 years.

John Doss, Buckingham Co., aged 85 years, residing with Rane Walker.

William Duval, Buckingham Co., aged 92 years, residing with Major William Duval.

James Wilkerson, Buckingham Co., aged 85 years, residing with Archibald Drinkard.

William Bigbie, Buckingham Co., aged 83 years.

John Preble, Campbell Co., aged 84 years.

Thomas P. Franklin, Campbell Co., aged 76 years.

John Cobbs, Campbell Co., aged 80 years.
Jesse Rice, Campbell Co., aged 80 years.
Isham Hall, Campbell Co., aged 90 years.
John Willard, Campbell Co., aged 84 years.
Edward Herndon, Campbell Co., aged 87 years.
General Joel Leftwich, Lynchburg, aged 80 years, residing with Rug Leftwich.
Arthur Litchford, Lynchburg, aged 82 years.
Richard Daniel, Lynchburg, aged 92 years.
David Calleham, Lynchburg, aged 82 years.
Sampson Evans, Lynchburg, aged 89 years.
James Brooks, Lynchburg, aged 85 years.
Thomas Franklin, Lynchburg, aged 83 years.
Harry Walthal, Lynchburg, 79 years.
Samuel Mathews, Lynchburg, aged 77 years.
James Howard, Lynchburg, aged 75 years.
James Whitaker, Lynchburg, aged 77 years.
Daniel Atkinson, Caroline Co., aged 89 years.
James Bradley, Caroline Co., aged 89 years.
William Coates, Caroline Co., aged 85 years.
Patrick Carnall, Caroline Co., aged 80 years.
William Gatewood, Caroline Co., aged 76 years.
Edmund Gatewood, Caroline Co., aged 78 years.
William Madison, Caroline Co., aged 75 years.
Betsy Perry, Caroline Co., aged 72 years.
Moses Stanly, Caroline Co., aged 82 years.
Robert Satterwhite, Caroline Co., aged 87 years.

(To be continued)

EARLY SETTLERS IN VIRGINIA.

(Continued from Vol. VI., page 152)

Addams, George (servant), tr. by Capt. Francis Epes, 26 Aug. 1635.

Agas, Edward, tr. by Edmund Scarborough, Accomac Co., 28 Nov., 1635.

Adkins, Christopher, tr. by Capt. William Peirce, 22 June 1635.

Aldman, Thomas, tr. by Rev. George White, 3 June, 1635.

Allen, Edward (servant), tr. by William Stone, Accomac Co., 4 June, 1635.

Alleson, Ann, tr. in the "Africa," grant to Capt. Adam Thorogood, 24 June, 1635.

Allin, William, tr. by Capt. William Peirce, 22 June, 1635.

Altmore, Thomas, tr. in the "John and Dorothy," 1635, by Capt. Thomas Thorogood.

Alporte, John, tr. in the "John and Dorothy," 1634, by Capt. Adam Thorogood.

Ames, Edward (servant), tr. by Capt. Francis Epes, 26 August, 1635.

Andrews, William, tr. by William Barker, 26 Nov., 1635.

Andrews, Susanna, wife of William Andrews of Accomac, tr. by him, 25 June, 1635.

Andrews, Thomas, tr. by George Menifie, 2 July, 1635.

Appleton, Richard, tr. by George Menefie, 2 July, 1635.

Aram, John (servant), tr. by Anthony Jones, 2 June, 1635.

Arnall, Robert (servant), tr. by William Spencer, 19 June, 1635.

Arnall, William (servant), tr. in 1621 by Edward Waters of Elizabeth City.

Arvine, John, county of Warrosquoicke, for his transportation, his wife Marie and son William, granted 6 June, 1635.

Ascough, Richard, tr. by Silvester Tolman, 21 July, 1635.

Ashby, Thomas, tr. by Jeremiah Clement, 22 June, 1635.

Asheley, Peter (servant), tr. by John Robins in the "Margaret and John" in 1622.

Ashton, Thomas, tr. by Jenkin Osborne, 9 July, 1635.

Atkins, Richard, came in "Abigail" in 1621, and said Atkins' wife came in "Tyger" in 1621.

Atkins, William, tr. by Capt. Adam Thorogood, 24 June, 1635.

Atwell, Isabell, tr. by Doctoris Christmas of Elizabeth City, 21 Nov., 1635.

Bagnal, Roger, tr. by John Upton, 7 July, 1635.

Baker, John, tr. by George Menifie, 2 July, 1635.

Baker, John (servant), tr. by Capt. Francis Epes, 26 Aug., 1635.

Banks, Richard, tr. by Lieut. John Cheesman of Charles River county, 21 Nov., 1635.

Banister, Stephen, tr. by John Sparkes, 3 June, 1635.

Banton, Thomas, tr. by John Parrott, 24 May, 1635.

Barle, Francis (servant), tr. by William Spencer, 19 June, 1635.

Barloe, Timothy, tr. by Capt. Thomas Willoughby, 19 Nov., 1635.

Barnards, John, tr. by Capt. Adam Thorogood, 24 June, 1635.

Barnett, Nicholas, tr. by William Swann of James City, 5 Nov. 1635.

Barren, Richard, tr. of John Moone, 21 Oct., 1635.

Bartwith, Robert, tr. by Capt. Thomas Willoughby, 19 Nov., 1635.

Bateman, Thomas, tr. by Jenkin Osborne, 9 July, 1635.

Bauchees, John (servant), tr. by Thomas Gray, James City, 27 August, 1635.

Beard, Joane, wife of William Beard, James City, tr. 19 June, 1635.

Belly, James, tr. in the "Bona Adventure" by Capt. Adam Thorogood, 24 June, 1635.

Bell, William, tr. by Thomas Harwood, 7 July, 1635.

Bellow, Thomas, tr. by William Pilkinton, 10 July, 1635.

Bennett, Ambrose, tr. by Richard Bennett, 26 June, 1635.

Bennett, Nicholas, tr. by William Clarke, Elizabeth City, 18 Nov., 1635.

Bennett, Robert, tr. by Capt. Adam Thorogood, 18 Dec., 1635.

Bennett, Robert (servant), tr. by John Slaughter, 30 May, 1635.

Bentley, William, planter of Elizabeth City, came over at his own charge in the "Jacob," 1624.

Bernard, Stephen, tr. by Capt. Adam Thorogood, 24 June, 1635.

Bilbie, Margaret, tr. in the "Hopewell," 1628, by Capt. Adam Thorogood.

Bird, Richard, tr. by Richard Bennett, 26 June, 1635.

Bird, William (servant), tr. by James Merriman of Charles City, 6 Nov., 1635.

Bishopp, John (servant), tr. by Thomas Gray of James City, 27 August, 1635.

Biss, William (servant), tr. by William Stone, Accomac Co., 4 June, 1635.

Blackstone, John (servant), tr. by William Stone, Accomac Co., 4 June, 1635.

Blacock, Robert, tr. in the "Bona Adventure" by Capt. Adam Thorogood, 24 June, 1635.

Boods, John, tr. by William Wilkinson, minister, 20 Nov., 1635.

Borne, Elizabeth (servant), tr. by Robert Sheppard, 19 July, 1635.

Boulton, Ann, tr. in the "Bona Adventure" by Capt. Adam Thorogood, 24 June, 1635.

Boulton, Thomas, tr. in the "Hopewell" in 1628 by Capt. Adam Thorogood.

Bowyer, Andrew, tr. in the "Truelove" in 1628 by Capt. Adam Thorogood.

Box, Anthony (servant), tr. by Capt. Francis Epes, 26 August, 1635.

Boyer, Thomas, tr. by Nathaniel Hooke, 5 June, 1635.

Bradston, John, tr. by Capt. Adam Thorogood, 24 June, 1635.

Brannly, Francis, tr. in the "Ark" by Capt. Adam Thorogood, 24 June, 1635.

Braunes, Blanch, tr. by Thomas Harwood, 7 July, 1635.

Brewer, Jeffrey, tr. by Thomas Shippey, 14 Nov., 1635.

Brewton, John, tr. in the "John and Dorothy," 1634, by Capt. Adam Thorogood.

Bridges, Thomas, tr. by William Barker, 26 Nov., 1635.

Brill, Peter, tr. by Sergt. Thomas Crompe of James Co., 25 Sept., 1635.

Brinchley, Michael (servant), tr. by Anthony Jones, 2 June, 1635.

Brinton, John, tr. by John Seaward, 1 July, 1635.

Brock, William, tr. by Jenkin Osborne, 9 July, 1635.

Bromley, Daniel, tr. by William Barker, 26 Nov., 1635.

Brooke, Thomas, tr. by Thomas Shippey, 14 Nov., 1635.

Berry, Richard, tr. by William Jones, Snr., Nansemond, Co., 7 November, 1700.

Brooke, William, tr. in the "Temperance," 1621, by Lieut. Thomas Flint.

Brookes, Cuthbert, tr. in the "Southampton" in 1622 by John Cheeseman, Elizabeth City.

Brooks, George, tr. by William Barker, 26 Nov., 1635.

Brooks, Thomas, tr. by Capt. Adam Thorogood, 24 June, 1635.

Brotherton, Dennis, tr. by Samuel Weaver, 2 July, 1635.

Browne, Elizabeth (servant), tr. by William Gany, Accomac Co., 17 Sept., 1635.

Browne, Robert (servant), tr. by William Gany, Accomac Co., 17 Sept., 1635.

Browne, Robert (servant), tr. by Thomas Gray, James City, 27 August, 1635.

Browne, Thomas (servant), tr. by George Holmes, 4 Aug., 1635.

Browne, William (servant), tr. by Richard Minter, 22 July, 1635.

Browning, George, tr. by Hugh Cox, 6 December, 1634.

Browning, John, tr. by Capt. William Peirce, 22 June, 1635.

Betts, William, and wife Barbara, tr. by William Major of New Kent. Co., 7 Nov., 1700.

Bryan, Edward (servant), tr. in 1620 by Edward Waters of Elizabeth City.

Bryant, John, tr. by Capt. William Peirce, 22 June, 1635.

VIRGINIA COUNTY RECORDS 57

Buck, Peter (servant), tr. by John Jackson, 9 June, 1635.
Bugbye, John, tr. by George Minifie, 2 July, 1635.
Bulmer, Bevis, tr. by Thomas Bagwell, 7 Nov., 1635.
Burcher, William (servant), tr. by William Stone, Accomac
Co., 4 June, 1635.
Burgess, John, tr. by Capt. Adam Thorogood, 18 Dec., 1635.
Burnett, Elizabeth (servant), tr. by Charles Harmar, 4 July,
1635.
Burnett, John, tr. by David Mansell, 22 July, 1635.
Burr, Edward, tr. by John Upton, 7 July, 1635.
Burroughs, Ann, tr. by Capt. Adam Thorogood, 24 June, 1635.
Burroughs, William, tr. by Capt. Adam Thorogood, 24 June,
1635.
Burrows, Matt., tr. by Thomas Harwood, 7 July, 1635.
Burpott, Richard, tr. by Christ. Woodward, ——, 1635.
Burtlock, George, tr. by David Mansell, 22 July, 1635.
Bush, Elizabeth, wife of John Bush of Elizabeth City, gent.,
and her two daughters, Elizabeth and Mary Bush, came in
the "Guift" in 1619.
Busher, Michael, tr. by Rev. Willis Heyley of Mulberry Island,
8 Dec., 1635.

(To be continued)

RICHMOND COUNTY WILLS.

(Continued from Vol. VI., page 230)

Travers, Rawleigh, Parish of Farnham. 20 Feb., 1701—4
March, 1701. To cousin Elizabeth Travers; to cousin
Winifred Travers; to cousin Rebecca Travers; to godson
Rawleigh Brooks; to my wife Sarah; Captain Thomas
Beale and my brother John Taverner to be executors; to
Mrs. Peachey, Mrs. Slaughter and Mrs. Sarah Baylis
each a ring; to Doctor Robert Clarke and Edward Jones;
Mr. Samuel Peachey; my sister Beale. Witnesses: Samuel
Peachey, Robert Clarke and Edward Jones.

Grady, Elizabeth, County of Richmond. 10 March, 1693-4—4 November, 1702. To Mary Smoot, daughter of William Smoot; William Smoot to be executor. Witnesses: Thomas Durham, Richard Draper and John Rankin.

Strothers, William, Senior, County of Richmond. 30 December, 1700—4 November, 1702. To my eldest son William after his mother's decease; my sons James, Robert and Benjamin; my son Joseph to be put to school; my grandson William Strother; my wife Dorothy and son James to be executors. Witnesses: James Phillips, Edward Langedell and William Smith.

Suttle, Henry, Parish of Farnham. 9 September, 1701—2 December, 1702. To John How; to my son Henry Suttle when he comes to the age of fourteen years; my wife Mary and the child she now goes with; my wife to be executrix. Witnesses: Elizabeth Suttle and John Doyle.

Jesper, Richard, Parish of Farnham. 11 June, 1698—3 March, 1702. My son Thomas Jesper and John Thomas to be executors; son Richard, my daughter Sara when she comes to the age of sixteen years; my two grandchildren William and Mary Dudley. Witnesses: William Lee, Mary Lee and Henry Hayes.

White, Richard, Parish of Sittenburn. 5 February, 1702—2 June, 1703. My godson Bryon, son of William Sisson; godson Richard, son of Edward Jones; my wife Katherine to be executrix. Witnesses: William Talbot and John Doyle.

Baylis, Sarah, Parish of North Farnham. 8 March, 1699-1700—2 June, 1703. My son John Suggitt; my son Edgecomb Suggitt; my son Thomas Suggitt; my son James Suggitt to be executor. Witnesses: John Sherdon, Joan Talbot and John Hughes.

Siges, John. 21 August, 1702—2 June, 1703. To Sam. Walten; to John and Thomas Walten; to my children; my wife to be executrix. Witnesses: John Key, Samuel Walton, John Walton and Mary Powell.

Walker, Thomas, aged about 59 years. Dated 31 January, 1702—7 July, 1703. My son Thomas Walker; my son William Walker; to Elizabeth Williams; to Shedderick Williams; to daughter Sarah; to Mary Walker; to Rachel Walker, my daughter; to Alice Walker, my daughter; my wife Anna. Witnesses: Lewis Richards, George Richards and James Grahame.

Powell, Pythagoras. 29 October, 1702—7 July, 1703. To my wife Sarah all my estate; Charles Snead to assist her as overseer. Witnesses: Alexander Rigges and Mary Spoo.

Loyd, Joane. 8 January, 1703—2 February, 1703. To daughter Susanna, wife of William Phillips; to son Shadrack Williams; to daughter Anne, wife of James Debard; to daughter Ruth, wife of John Canterbury; to granddaughter Elizabeth Thornhill; daughter-in-law Elizabeth Williams; to son-in-law George Thompson; to granddaughter Susan Phillips; to grandson John McDaniel; to son-in-law William Phillips; son-in-law George Thompson to be executor. Witnesses: Robert Thomas, Deborah Thomas and William Yates.

Hefford, Zachary. 30 September, 1703—2 February, 1703. To daughter Mary, wife of William Taylor; to son John of the age of fourteen years; to son Zachary of the age of four years; friend John Pound, Snr., to be executor. Witnesses: John Pound, Jnr., Edmund Neall and John Charteris.

Williams, Henry, Parish of North Farnham. 25 January, 1703-4—1 March, 1703. To my wife Lettie; to daughter Mary, the wife of Phillip Harris, and their daughter Sarah; to son John Williams; to son Thomas Williams; to daughter Sarah Williams; to daughter Jane Williams; son John to be Executor. Witnesses: Andrew Dew and Henry Jennings.

Gilbert, James. 1 January, 1701—7 January, 1704. To my wife; my friend John Mills, Jnr., to be executor. Witnesses: Edward Welch, Jone Williams and Thomas White.

Duzen, Thomas, County of Rappahannock, Parish of Farnham. 6 August, 1691—7 January, 1704. Estate to wife Susanna, and she to be executrix. Witnesses: William Smith, James Rawlin and Charles Dodson.

Woffendall, Adam. 25 April, 1703—7 January, 1704. To my sons Harris and Strother; my daughter Sarah; my daughter Mary; my son Francis; my wife to be executrix. Witnesses: John Grimsley, Thomas Arnold and Andrew Harrison.

Sutherne, Thomas. 17 April, 1704—2 August, 1704. My son Thomas; my wife Elinor and her three daughters; my sons William and James; my daughter-in-law Mary Sutherne; my wife to be executrix. Witnesses: Christopher Petty, Richard Dodson and Charles Dodson, Snr.

Nayler, Avery. 24 January, 1704-5—7 March, 1704-5. My wife Patience; godson Avery, son of Arthur Die; my wife to be executrix. Witnesses: Seaburn Pinkett, James Murphy and Stephen Huchisson.

Samford, James. 27 September, 1703—2 November, 1704. To my grandson Thomas Samford; my grandson James Samford; to the rest of the children of my son Samuel Samford; mentions land bequeathed by Thomas Samford to grandson James Samford; to Elizabeth, wife of son Samuel Samford; to grandsons William Giles and John Samford; to Samford Jones; to grandson William Samford; to Edward Jones; son Samuel to be executor. Witnesses: Giles Webb, Richard Taylor and Edward Jones.

Suggitt, John, gentleman. 16 January, 1703—7 March, 1704. To daughter Elizabeth Suggitt; to brother James Suggitt; to brother Edgecomb Suggitt; to Thomas Ayres; to William Ayres; to William Smith, my brother-in-law; to brother Thomas Suggitt; to Robert Clarke; my wife and my brother Thomas Suggitt to be executors. Witnesses: Robert Clarke and James Murphy.

Gwyn, David. 22 February, 1702-3—8 March, 1704. To my two daughters Elizabeth Gwyn and Sarah Gwyn; my daughter Katherine Gwyn; my sister Elizabeth Gwyn, wife to Mr. Benjamin Gwyn of Bristol; my brother Edward Gwyn, clerk in Wales; my wife Katherine; to sister Mary my estate in Wales lying near Harford West; my son-in-law William Fauntleroy; my son-in-law Moore Fauntleroy; my son-in-law Griffin; my wife to be executrix. Witnesses: William Taylor, James Sherlock and Thomas Beale.

Horneby, Daniel, Parish of North Farnham. 24 August, 1705 —5 September, 1705. To my son Daniel; to daughter Frances; to Thomas Barlow; son Daniel to be executor; friends Mr. John Taverner and Mr. Thomas Suggitt to be overseers. Witnesses: Thomas Barlow and Henry Jennings.

Bradley, Thomas. 9 July, 1705—5 September, 1705. To Elizabeth Smith; my wife Elizabeth to be executrix. Witnesses: Jonathan Gilbert, John Kelly and William Shaw.

Teboe, Charles, Parish of St. Mary's. 3 February, 1704—3 October, 1705. My wife Frances to be executrix; daughter Jeane Teboe; daughter Sarah; daughter Anne; eldest son Charles; daughter Frances Teboe; daughter Martha; son John. Witnesses: William Marshall, Lewis Jones and Richard Tankersley.

Tillery, Thomas. 19 June, 1705—3 October, 1705. To my son Job; my brother Job Tillery; my wife Sarah to be executrix. Witnesses: Thomas Jenkins and James Coward.

Smith, Eve, Parish of North Farnham. 24 April, 1704—4 October, 1705. My grandsons William Goad and John Goad; my daughter Katherine Goad to have her father John Williams' chest; granddaughter Hannah Goad; son Abraham Goad to be executor. Witnesses: William Dodson, Charles Dodson, Snr., and Anne Dodson.

(To be continued)

RAPPAHANNOCK COUNTY WILLS.

(Continued from Vol. VI., page 220)

Etherington, Margaret, widow.   15 Feb., 1682—4 March, 1684-5.   Three sons John and William Jennings and Christopher Etherington; son John Jennings, executor. Witnesses: Francis Stone, Elizabeth Stone.

Herbert, Thomas.   8 Jan., 1684-5—1 April, 1685.   Cousin John Waters, Snr., sole executor.   Witnesses: Elizabeth Newton, Frances Moss, William Jones.

King, James.   24 Jan., 1684—2 May, 1685.   Eldest son John Loflin; son Robert King; John Mills, executor. Witnesses: Thomas New, Robert Webber.

Waters, Roger.   8 April, 1685—6 May, 1685.   Mrs. Ann Glascock; Frances Glascock; John Ockley, Snr. and Jnr.; Nicholas Clark; Michael Scarlock; Thomas Glascock, executor; Dr. Dacres to preach the funeral sermon.   Witnesses: John Ockley, Nicholas Clark.

Barrow, John.   3 Feb., 1684—6 May, 1685.   Sons Jonathan, Alexander and Moses; daughters Honor and Cicely; wife Mary and son Alexander, executors; William Underwood, Snr., and John Burkett, overseers.   Witnesses: Wm. Underwood, Snr., Wm. Underwood, Jnr., Jane Underwood.

Carden, Robert.   18 Feb., 1684-5—6 May, 1685.   Son Robert to live with Humphrey Davis and his wife until he is seventeen years; wife Elizabeth executrix.   Witnesses: Thomas Parker, Will Jones.

Richards, Bridget.   10 April, 1685—24 May, 1685.   Husband Lewis Richards; daughter Ann Pridum; son Christopher Pridum; my four children.   Witnesses: Thomas Walker, William Sisson.

Putlee, Nicholas.   18 April, 1685—4 June, 1685.   Wife Mary; to orphan boy named Peter Gansallow a mare foal.   Witnesses: Anthony Forbes, Robert Mills, John King.

Moss, William, Snr.   21 April, 1685—22 July, 1685.   Son William executor; daughter Frances; daughter Elizabeth;

brother Robert Moss; Edward Westbury; Thomas New. Witnesses: Robert Moss, Elias Wilson, Thomas New.

Coghill, James. 5 Oct., 1684—1 Sept., 1685. Sons James, Frederick and David; daughters Margaret and Mary; wife Mary executrix. Witnesses: Thomas Offenle, Christopher Man.

Reynolds, Cornelius. 29 Sept., 1684—4 Nov., 1685. Wife Margaret executrix; sons William and John; grandson Goss. Witnesses: Thomas Hope, Mary Hope, Matt. Lafry.

Sampson, John, merchant. 7 Sept., 1680—25 Nov., 1685. Sister Rebecca Sampson; Mrs. Sarah Suggett; brothers Jacob and Isaac Sampson; John Taverner; my father Ptolomeus Sampson of Tattons; brother Isaac Sampson in London; John Suggett executor.

Jones, Honoria, relict of George Jones. 9 Nov., 1685—21 Dec., 1685. Daughter Margaret Blagg; daughter Elizabeth Gardiner my ring which joined me and my husband Major John Weire in matrimony; son-in-law Abraham Blagg; son Richard Gardiner; grandson Richard Watts; grandson Edward Blagg; grandson Abraham Blagg; grandson Luke Gardiner; grandson John Gardiner; daughter Margaret, wife of Abraham Blagg, to be executrix. Witnesses: James Harrison, Michael Bassey.

Boyess, George. 8 Jan., 1685-6—3 Feb., 1685-6. Frances, daughter of John Dangerfield; Jeremiah, son of Thomas Parker; sister Dorothy Boyess executrix; goddaughter Sarah, daughter of Daniel Shipley; estate to be managed by John Dangerfield until my sister arrives from England. Witnesses: Thomas Parker, Daniel Shipley, Alice Shipley.

Yeats, James. 9 Jan., 1685—3 March, 1685-6. Friend William Clapham executor. Witnesses: Thomas Haire, Rowland Thornton, John Jackson.

Godson, Frances. 27 Jan., 1685-6—7 April, 1686. To Toby and Henry Smith; Mrs. Elizabeth Smith. Witnesses: Gerard Fitzgerald, Edward Adcock.

64   VIRGINIA COUNTY RECORDS

Bowen, John. 1 April, 1686—15 May, 1686. Sons Matthew,
John, Stephen and Alexander; daughter Martha; my wife
and child she goes with; wife and son Matthew executors.
Witnesses: Moses Hulbert, Alexander Doniphan, Francis
Williams.

Willoughby, Henry. 28 Oct., 1685—21 Dec., 1686. Daughter
Rebecca Hull; granddaughters Sarah and Margaret Hull;
daughter to be executrix.

Gibson, Magdalen. 7 Sept., 1685—4 Aug., 1686. Son Tobias
Ingram and his first child; Arabella White; son and John
Gray executors. Witnesses: Thomas Parker, Nathaniel
Allen.

Palmer, John. 16 Sept., 1686—18 Oct., 1686. William Barber
executor; my wife in England; John Peterson. Witnesses: Ralph Graydon, John Welch, John Peterson.

Page, Jonas. 22 July, 1686—28 Oct., 1686. Henry Clarke
executor; Henry Clarke, Jnr. Witnesses: Richard Dudley, Henry Tillery, Thomas Dudley.

Fuller, Thomas. 11 Jan., 1685-1686—3 Nov., 1686. Daughter
Susanna; William Witt; my wife. Witnesses: John Haw-
ford, Zachariah Hefford.

Rice, Ann, relict of Dominick Rice. 8 Feb., 1684-5—3 Nov.,
1686. Son Thomas Due executor, and I leave all my children to his care; daughter Ann Toone. Witnesses: Joseph
Jefferson, Samuel Whitehead.

Gubb, Nathaniel. 20 Nov., 1686—5 Jan., 1686-7. Sister
Michah; my mother executrix, and after her decease to
my cousins; Mr. Joseph Haringer; Mr. Joseph Robinson,
attorney-at-law. Witnesses: James Hanford, Henry Taylor.

Lincoln, John. 18 Dec., 1686—5 Jan., 1686-7. Wife Elizabeth; son John; daughters Elizabeth, Margaret and Catherine; Charles Dodford executor. Witnesses: Henry
Hartley, John Mills, Gilbert Croswell.

Withers, John. 2 April, 1686—5 Jan., 1686-7. Daughter Margaret Withers; wife Sarah and child she goes with; wife executrix. Witnesses: Thomas Kendall, John Crow, William Heather.

Billington, Luke. 25 Jan., 1686—2 March, 1686-7. To Teige McDonough; William Robinson; Ann Robinson. Witnesses: Tiege McDonough, Lawrence Hennings.

Tayler, Thomas. 22 Jan., 1686—2 March, 1686-7. Godsons John Tavener, Jnr., and Sanford Jones; Isaac, son of John Webb; Rees Evans; Thomas White; Elizabeth Pond; my boy servant Thomas Hewett; friends Edward and Mrs. Jones; Thomas Baylis; Catherine Baylis; James Sanford and William Orlston executors. Witnesses: Isaac Webb, John Blake, James Davis.

Cauthorne, Richard. 18 March, 1679-80—2 March, 1686-7. Eldest son Richard; son Thomas; wife Ann executrix. Witnesses: Edmund Crask, Robert Gullock.

Travers, William. 14 Feb., 1686-7—2 March, 1686-7. Mother Rebecca Rice; brothers Samuel and Rawleigh Travers; father-in-law John Rice; Samuel, son of Elias Robinson; my two brothers executors. Witnesses: William Slaughter, George Baker, Joanna Grayson.

Johnston, Edward, Farnham Parish. 29 Jan., 1686-7—2 March, 1686-7. William Macanico, heifers on plantation of Ennis Macanico; Charles Dodson executor. Witnesses: Daniel Everard, Alexander Duke, Peter Elmore.

Parker, Robert, planter, Sittingbourne Parish. 15 Jan., 1686-7—2 March, 1686-7. My wife and four children; son John; wife executrix. Witnesses: Edward Keeling, Caleb Lyon.

FAMILY HISTORY.
MORTON OF AMELIA COUNTY.

Conveyance from Joseph Morton of Amelia to Edward Osborne of same county, planter, a tract of land in Amelia which was granted to said Morton by patent. Recorded 14 July, 1738. Book 1, page 87.

Joseph Morton, Jnr., of Amelia to John Nash of Henrico county, 1000 acres in Amelia county. Agnes, wife of said Joseph Morton, relinquished her dower rights, 8 Dec., 1738. Book —, page 108.

Thomas Morton of Amelia county to John Short of James City county, 126 acres in Amelia. 1 June, 1740. Book 1, page 164.

Elizabeth Morton of Henrico county to son Thomas Morton, a tract of land in Amelia county, 59 acres, being a patent granted to said Elizabeth Morton 1 August, 1734, joining the land given said Thomas by his father's will bearing date 9 Feb., 1730-1 ; and I also grant to my son John 159 acres in said county, formerly granted to me by patent; also to my beloved daughter Ann Gathwright, now wife of William Gathwright of the county of Henrico, 159 acres; also I give to my daughter Judith Morton 159 acres in said county; also to Samuel Morton, my nephew, son of John Morton of county of Henrico, 159 acres. Dated 20 Sept., 1740. Witness, Richard Morton. Book 1, page 200.

Conveyance from Joseph Morton, Snr., of Amelia to Joseph Mackgehee of said county, 400 acres in said county. Elizabeth, wife of Joseph Morton, relinquishing her dower. 15 Jan., 1741. Book 1, page 255.

Joseph Morton Snr., of Brunswick county to Thomas Morton of Amelia, 225 acres in latter county. 15 Feb., 1744. Book 2, page 49.

Richard Morton of Amelia county to Thomas Brackett of Goochland county, 150 acres in Amelia county. 19 April, 1746. Book 2, page 155.

Samuel Morton of the county of Amelia to Edward Good of Henrico county, 121 acres in Amelia. 28 Oct., 1747. Book 2, page 245.

Conveyance from Thomas Morton and John Morton, Jnr., of Amelia to Thomas Brackett of Cumberland county, 573 acres in Amelia. 6 Sept., 1751. Book 4, page 66.

Richard Morton of Amelia to William Archer of same county, 2 tracts of land. Mentions his sister Judith Good and his cousin Samuel Morton. 23 Sept., 1751. Book 4, page 67.

Conveyance from Joseph Morton of Amelia to his daughter Mary Price, wife of William Price of Amelia, 250 acres in said county. 14 Sept., 1750. Witnesses: Josiah Morton, Stephen Morton. Book 4, page 216.

Joseph Morton and Agnes, his wife, parish of Nottoway, county of Amelia, planter to Walter Douglas of Hanover county, 950 acres in Amelia. 23 May, 1753. Josiah Morton, witness. Book 4, page 254.

FAMILY HISTORY.

ANDERSON OF HANOVER COUNTY.

Nathaniel Anderson and Bartelot Anderson, witnesses to act of renunciation of Mary Clayton to the right of taking out letters of administration on the estate of her late husband Arthur Clayton. Recorded 4 Jan., 1733. Vol. 1, page 2.

Conveyance from James Robertson of St. Martin's Parish, Hanover, planter to Matthew Anderson of St. Paul's Parish, same county, gent., 1326 acres in St. Martin's Parish. 4 Jan., 1733. Vol. 1, page 6.

John Nuckolds of St. Martin's Parish, Hanover, to Ponncey Anderson of aforesaid parish and county, a parcel of land with plantation on it in said county. Witnesses: Nelson Anderson, Anthony Metcalf. 1 Feb., 1733. Vol. 1, page 20.

Mary Anderson of St. Paul's Parish, Hanover, relict and surviving executrix of Robert Anderson, late of New Kent county, now Hanover. Whereas, said deceased by his last will and testament, proved in New Kent, did give and bequeath unto his son John Anderson, now of parish and county of Hanover, 30 pounds to buy him a tract of land, the said Mary Anderson for love and affection she bears to her son John Anderson conveys to him a tract of land with plantation thereon containing 335 acres, which was bought of George Wilkinson as by deeds bearing date 13 and 14 Jan., 1719, and acknowledged in the Court of New Kent 14 Jan., 1719, lying in St. Paul's Parish, Hanover, adjacent to the upper moiety of said land purchased of said Wilkinson which is to be my son Charles Anderson's, conveyed to him by deed bearing date with these presents. Witnesses: Thomas Crenshaw, Richard Lancaster, Sarah Harris, Bartelot Anderson. 5 April, 1734.

Mary Anderson of St. Paul's Parish, Hanover county, to her son Charles Anderson for 30 pounds currency as left him in the will of his father Robert Anderson, late of New Kent county, etc. (see preceding deed), 335 acres in Hanover county. 5 April, 1734. Vol. 1, page 36.

Matthew Anderson of St. Paul's Parish, Hanover county, merchant, to James Power of James City Parish and county, 1126 acres in St. Martin's Parish, Hanover county. 22 July, 1734. Vol. 1, page 162.

John Anderson of Hanover county to his brother Nathaniel Anderson of same place, 1 acre in said county being a moiety of a tract which Mary Anderson bought of George Wilkinson and which she conveyed to said John Anderson by deed bearing date 23 March, 1733. Recorded 3 July, 1735. Vol. 1, page 279.

Sarah Anderson, widow of John Anderson, late of the Parish of St. Paul, Hanover county, gent., decd., and John Anderson of same parish and county, planter, to John Thomson of same place, merchant, for 10 pounds currency, 80 acres, being the same land which by deed poll from Samuel Waddy, dated 28 Jan., 1696, was conveyed to said John Anderson, gent., and Sarah, his wife, and the heirs of her body, which heir the said John Anderson, party to these presents, is. 7 August, 1735. Vol. 1, page 287.

Nelson Anderson, bond as guardian of Robert Anderson, orphan of David Anderson, decd., 100 pounds. 4 Sept., 1735. Vol. 1, page 330.

Richard Anderson of Bedford county and Elizabeth, his wife, to Elijah Priddy of Hanover county, 200 acres in latter county, bounded by the lands of Edward Lankford, Stephen Stone, Mansfield and Francis Clark. Witnesses: John Priddy, Snr., William Anderson, Bartelot Anderson and Charles Anderson. 8 March, 1783. Vol. 2, page 44.

Richard Clough Anderson, late of Hanover county, Virginia, but at present of Jefferson county, Kentucky, power of attorney to his brother Mathew Anderson, dated 8 August, 1784, at Louisville, Ky. At a Court held for Hanover county, 6 Jan., 1785.

FAMILY HISTORY.

LANIER OF BRUNSWICK COUNTY.

Brunswick county, Va. At a Court held 6th of July, 1732, Nicholas Lanear petitioned the court for a crop mark, and same is admitted to record.

Court held 2 Nov., 1732. The following were represented to the Governor as being fit for the Commission of the Peace: John Duke, Batle Peterson, Nicholas Lanier, Wm. Hagood and Thomas Wilson, gentlemen.

Court held 6 Feb., 1734. Nicholas Lanier, gentleman, appointed overseer of a bridle path from his house to this Court House.

At a Court held 2 Oct., 1734. Byrd Lanier is appointed overseer of the new road to Shining Creek.

Deed made 3rd July, 1740. "William Martin gives to daughter Anne Lanier, wife of Thomas Lanier, consideration natural affection, etc., 236 acres of land on Isinglass Creek, it being part of the patent to me in 1726."

Court held 5 July, 1733. Nicholas Lanier and others sworn as Justices by virtue of a Commission from the Hon. Wm. Gooch, Lt.-Gov., dated 14 June, 1730.

Court held 4 Dec., 1735. Byrd Thomas Lanier is appointed constable instead of James McDaniel.

Court held 2 March, 1737. Wm. Martin, Nicholas Lanier and John Duke, gentlemen, are recommended to the Governor as fit persons out of whom to appoint a Sheriff for the county for the ensuing year.

Court held 2 Feb., 1738. Thomas Lanier, with others, recommended as Justices.

Court held 6 March, 1739. John Duke, Nicholas Lanier and Wm. Hagood, gents., are recommended as persons fit to execute office of Sheriff for ensuing year.

Court held 5 March, 1740. Nicholas Lanier, gent., appointed Justice and took the oath. At same Court Nicholas Lanier recommended for Sheriff.

Court held 2 July, 1741. Nicholas Lanier, gent., Captain of a company of Foot, produced his commission for his post in the Militia of this county.

Court held 3 July, 1741. Thomas Lanier, Lieutenant of company of Foot in Militia of this county, took the oath.

Court held 5 March, 1741. Nicholas Lanier, gent., and others recommended for Sheriff for the ensuing year.

Court held 5 June, 1746. George Walton, Nicholas Lanier and Lewis Parham took oath as Justices.

Court held 7 Aug., 1746. Nicholas Lanier, gent., took oath as Captain of company of Foot.

Court held 4 Sept., 1746. Richard Lanier produced commission as Lieut. of company of Foot.

Court held 1st. Jan., 1746. Nicholas Lanier qualified as Justice.

Court held Oct., 1748. Richard Lanier produced commission as Lieut. of company of Foot.

Court held 4 Sept., 1751. Nicholas Lanier qualified as Justice.

Court held Nov., 1752. Sampson Lanier and Isaac Rowe Walton and others recommended as Justices.

Court held 24 July, 1753. Sampson Lanier qualified as justice.

Court held 23 July, 1754. Sampson Lanier qualified as Vestryman of Parish of St. Andrew's.

Court held 6 Sept., 1754. Richard Lanier, Lieut., qualified for the Militia.

Court held 26 August, 1755. Sampson Lanier qualified as Vestryman of St. Andrew's.

Court held 4 Feb., 1756. Commission to Sampson Lanier to qualify as Justice.

Court held 7 July, 1756. Sampson Lanier recommended as Sheriff.

Court held 26 April, 1757. Sampson Lanier one of committee to inspect Clerk's Office.

Court held 2 Sept., 1757. On motion of Elizabeth Lanier, widow of Sampson Lanier, decd., administratrix on his estate. Same granted, with John Pettaerny, Richard Burch and Samuel Lanier, her securities, same acknowledge bonds for $2,000.

Court held 22 Aug., 1756. Samuel Lanier recommended as Justice.

Court held 23 Nov., 1757. Burwell Lanier, orphan of Sampson Lanier, made choice of Samuel Lanier for his guardian.

Court same day. Elizabeth Lanier, widow of Sampson Lanier, assigned dower.

Court held 27 Feb., 1759. Rebecca Lanier, orphan of Sampson Lanier, makes choice of Cuthbert Smith as her guardian.

Court held 26 May, 1760. Lemuel Lanier appointed to make list of tithables in lower part of St. Andrew's Parish.

Court held 23 April, 1763. William Lanier appointed guardian to Lewis and Aggy Lanier, orphans of Sampson Lanier.

Court held 2 May, 1765. Cuthbert Smith appointed guardian to Nancy Lanier, orphan of Sampson Lanier, in the room of Lemuel Lanier, who is discharged.

Court held 27 July, 1767. License granted to Lewis Lanier to keep an ordinary at his own house. Wm. Lanier being his security.

Court held 27 Feb., 1769. Leave to Benjamin Lanier to erect a mill on Three Creeks.

Court held 26 Aug., 1771. Wm. Lanier made surveyor of Middle Church road.

Court held 23 March, 1772. Elizabeth Lanier, wife of Robert Lanier, relinquishes dower in land heretofore conveyed by said Robert to Thomas Mitchell.

Court held 23 Nov., 1772. Nicholas Lanier discharged from paying county levies for the future.

(To be continued)

Vol. VII   JUNE, 1910   Part 2

Virginia
County Records

PUBLISHED QUARTERLY

EDITED BY

William Armstrong Crozier, F. R. S., F. G. S. A.

Published by
The Genealogical Association
Hasbrouck Heights
New Jersey

Five Dollars a Year   Single Copies, Two Dollars

Virginia County Records

Published Quarterly

CONTENTS

Virginia County Records

QUARTERLY MAGAZINE

| VOL. VII | JUNE 1910 | No. 2 |

INDEX TO LAND GRANTS

ISLE OF WIGHT COUNTY.

Book No. 10.

97	Wm. Evans	1713	100
97	Wm. Arrington	1713	200
98	Francis Mayberry	1713	125
98	Richard Reynolds, Jr.	1713	200
98	Samuel Cornwell	1713	130
99	Thomas Drake	1713	250
99	Edward Boykin	1713	190
100	James Atkinson, Jr.	1713	250
101	Charles Jones	1713	185
101	Richard Blow	1713	100
101	Wm. Mayo	1713	220
102	Bridgman Joyner, Jr.	1713	270
102	Richard Drake	1713	285
103	Edward Stephens	1713	230
105	Lawrence Hunt	1713	200
106	John Drew	1713	420
106	Henry Pope	1713	195
106	Wm. Rose	1713	150
107	George Smith	1713	100
107	George Wyech	1713	150
108	John Denson	1713	230
108	Richard Drake	1713	200
108	Thomas Kerby	1713	350
109	Richard Williams	1713	400
109	Wm. Faircloth	1713	275
109	John Rasberry	1713	170
110	Henry Pope	1713	200
110	Robert Lanier	1713	225
111	John Barnes	1713	340
112	Wm. Hickman	1713	370
113	Robert Hodge	1713	500
113	John Hawthorn	1713	315
114	Arnold Pew	1713	270
114	Richard Renolds	1713	113
115	Edward Harris	1713	540
116	John Teasley	1713	200
117	Theophilus Joyner	1713	345

117	Martin Dawson	1713	350
119	Philip Rayford	1713	325
120	Benjamin Evans	1713	375
120	Thomas Drake	1713	230
124	Abraham Brawler	1713	340
127	Sarah Reddyhoe	1714	115
147	Barneby Macquinny	1714	490
130	Barneby Macquinny	1714	670
130	Thomas Jarrell	1714	200
130	Nicholas Cock and George Ezell	1714	190
116	Captn. John Allen	1713	240
131	Nathaniel Harrison	1714	1750
143	Wm. Edwards	1714	540
143	Saml. Harwood, Jr.	1714	445
146	Wm. Edwards	1714	120
145	Joseph Seward	1714	95
146	Bartholemew Andross	1714	320
146	Wm. Hinlim	1714	245
149	Francis Bressey	1714	240
149	Isabel Havield	1714	120
149	Edward Boykin	1714	160
149	Thomas Barrow	1714	100
150	Adam Heith, Jr.	1714	110
153	Henry Clarke	1714	100
154	Col. Thos. Godwin	1714	250
157	Chas. Jones	1714	230
164	Edward Jones	1714	215
164	Robert Rikes	1714	430
165	Cap. Henry Harrison and Philip Ludwell	1714	6365
168	Etheldred Taylor	1714	545
171	Thomas Jarrell, Jr. and Jos. Lane	1714	1400
172	Wm. Hunter	1714	225
174	Wm. Edwards	1714	1275
176	Same	1714	440
180	Wm. Gray, Jr.	1714	360
180	John Kelley	1714	125
182	Samuel Harwood, Jr.	1714	380

183	Edward Goodrich	1714	230
184	Wm. West	1714	400
184	Wm. Edwards	1714	570
192	Matthew Markes	1714	200
194	Walter Bailey	1714	240
195	Henry Briggs	1714	415
195	Wm. Crumpler	1714	270
196	Wm. Scott, Jr.	1714	1700
196	Edward Goodson and Matthew Ruslim	1714	475
196	Thomas Newscome	1714	180
200	Nicholas Williams	1714	200
200	Francis Bressy	1714	350
201	Richard Washington	1714	1240
201	Barneby Macquinny	1714	545
201	Bridgman Joyner	1714	800
201	John Parnell and Mary Jolly	1714	237
202	Richard Washington	1714	850
202	Same	1714	300
202	John Lawrence	1714	580
203	Thomas Blunt	1714	710
203	Joseph Lane	1714	150
222	Barneby Macquinny	1714	3435
223	Thomas Blunt	1714	420
223	Benjamin Chapman	1714	480
223	Wm. Brown	1714	325
224	Same	1714	430
224	Thomas Hart	1714	295
224	James Jones	1714	260
231	Philip Rayford	1714	525
234	Hinshea Guillum	1714	620
244	Samuel Brown	1715	200
254	Joseph Holt	1716	615
255	Same	1716	300
256	Arthur Davis	1715	170
256	Wm. Hinchin	1715	100
257	Hugh Matthews	1715	100
257	Thos. Smith	1715	85

VIRGINIA COUNTY RECORDS 77

<table>
<tr><td>257</td><td>Henry Pope</td><td>1715</td><td>85</td></tr>
<tr><td>257</td><td>Joseph Turner</td><td>1715</td><td>150</td></tr>
<tr><td>258</td><td>Randall Revell</td><td>1715</td><td>50</td></tr>
<tr><td>243</td><td>Charles Porter</td><td>1715</td><td>135</td></tr>
<tr><td>258</td><td>Hugh Lee</td><td>1715</td><td>100</td></tr>
<tr><td>258</td><td>Richard Blow</td><td>1715</td><td>110</td></tr>
<tr><td>258</td><td>John Baily</td><td>1715</td><td>150</td></tr>
<tr><td>258</td><td>John Vick</td><td>1715</td><td>100</td></tr>
<tr><td>259</td><td>Thomas Joyner</td><td>1715</td><td>150</td></tr>
<tr><td>259</td><td>Thomas Taylor</td><td>1715</td><td>150</td></tr>
<tr><td>259</td><td>John Watts</td><td>1715</td><td>65</td></tr>
<tr><td>259</td><td>Wm. Wilkason</td><td>1715</td><td>100</td></tr>
<tr><td>260</td><td>John Joyner</td><td>1715</td><td>225</td></tr>
<tr><td>261</td><td>John Rachell</td><td>1715</td><td>80</td></tr>
<tr><td>264</td><td>Wm. Rose, Jr.</td><td>1715</td><td>100</td></tr>
<tr><td>264</td><td>Arthur Kavenaugh</td><td>1715</td><td>175</td></tr>
<tr><td>267</td><td>Wm. Cain</td><td>1715</td><td>82</td></tr>
<tr><td>270</td><td>Wm. Edwards</td><td>1715</td><td>330</td></tr>
<tr><td>267</td><td>John Lear</td><td>1715</td><td>235</td></tr>
<tr><td>268</td><td>Robert Scott</td><td>1715</td><td>180</td></tr>
<tr><td>268</td><td>Andrew Griffin</td><td>1715</td><td>195</td></tr>
<tr><td>268</td><td>Wm. Scott, Jr.</td><td>1715</td><td>100</td></tr>
<tr><td>269</td><td>Thomas Jarrell</td><td>1715</td><td>90</td></tr>
<tr><td>269</td><td>Thomas Carter</td><td>1715</td><td>120</td></tr>
<tr><td>269</td><td>James Joyner</td><td>1715</td><td>118</td></tr>
<tr><td>270</td><td>v Wm. Brown</td><td>1715</td><td>100</td></tr>
<tr><td>270</td><td>Thomas Jarrell</td><td>1715</td><td>70</td></tr>
<tr><td>271</td><td>John Edwards</td><td>1715</td><td>90</td></tr>
<tr><td>271</td><td>Wm. Oudelant</td><td>1715</td><td>145</td></tr>
<tr><td>271</td><td>Edward Boykin</td><td>1715</td><td>145</td></tr>
<tr><td>272</td><td>Abraham Stephenson</td><td>1715</td><td>145</td></tr>
<tr><td>272</td><td>James Barnes</td><td>1715</td><td>100</td></tr>
<tr><td>272</td><td>Wm. Browne</td><td>1715</td><td>130</td></tr>
<tr><td>276</td><td>William Pope</td><td>1715</td><td>90</td></tr>
<tr><td>277</td><td>Hugh Golitely</td><td>1715</td><td>200</td></tr>
<tr><td>278</td><td>James Lundy</td><td>1715</td><td>290</td></tr>
<tr><td>279</td><td>John Peterson</td><td>1715</td><td>200</td></tr>
</table>

280	Wm. Batts	1715	250
280	John Poythress	1715	100
288	Josiah John Holliman	1715	50
291	Nehemiah Joyner	1716	100
306	John Denson	1716	295
308	James Thweat	1716	180
308	Richard Lewis	1716	150
308	Thomas Holliday	1716	120
303	John Simmons	1716	710
310	James Denson	1716	420
315	Richard Drake, Jr.	1716	200
315	Thomas Collyer	1716	440
326	Henry Beddingfield	1716	165
342	Owen Mirack	1716	180
342	Francis West	1716	132
343	John Baptis Curtsi	1716	100
343	John Persons	1716	76
344	John Wall	1716	100
354	James Mercer	1716	100
355	John Cain	1716	165
355	Theophilus Joyner	1716	385
356	Henry Pendry	1717	100
366	John Vauhan	1717	110
370	Thomas Allen	1717	195
371	Theophilus Joyner	1717	225
371	Jacob Summerlin	1717	150
372	Martin Middleton	1717	90
372	Edward Brantley	1717	400
381	John Guillam	1717	390
382	Giles Driver, Jr.	1717	230
410	John Simmons	1717	350
423	John Joyner	1719	350
423	Nathan Joyner	1719	225
425	William Batte	1719	170
425	Edward Brantley	1719	225
424	Thomas Brown	1719	125
424	James Binam	1719	100

424	Robert Little	1719	170
426	Benjamin Howard	1719	200
458	Richard Smith	1719	390
459	Thomas Smith	1719	270
459	Nicholas Smith	1719	100
460	William Auldridge	1719	100
460	John Peterson	1719	385
460	Same	1719	330
128	Thomas Hunt	1714	140

BOOK No. 11.

49	John Thweat	1720	135
56	Adam Ivy	1720	150
48	John Peterson	1720	100
56	Thomas Dunn	1720	200
56	Adam Ivy	1720	100
55	James Sammon	1720	170
55	Thomas Griffis	1720	100
137	Same	1722	400
137	John Pennington	1722	150
166	John Jones	1722	170
167	George Cornit	1722	90
167	Wm. Kinney	1722	400
167	John Branch	1722	200
168	Arthur Kavenaugh	1722	400
168	John Parsons	1722	130
169	Randall Revel	1722	75
169	Same	1722	85
170	John Scott and John Scott, Jr.	1722	100
170	John Scott	1722	145
171	Arthur Kavenaugh	1722	50
171	John Scott, Jr.	1722	180
171	John Golitely	1722	100
172	John Parsons	1722	100
172	Thomas Macey	1722	100
173	Thomas Moy	1722	100
173	Thomas Johnson	1722	185

136	John Mason	1722	250
174	Henry Powers	1722	250
174	Francis Regan	1722	165
175	Wm. Simmons	1722	425
175	Wm. Powell	1722	125
176	Francis Mirach	1722	250
248	Wm. Exum	1722	275
249v	John Chapman	1722	240
249	John Dawson	1722	100
250	John Drew	1722	270
193	James Davis	1722	330
193	Wm. Richardson	1722	300
251	John Bowin	1722	116
251	Rebeccah Howell	1722	100
251	Jos. John Bridger	1722	350
252	James Massingall	1722	265
252	Thomas Barrow	1722	225
253	Thomas Addeson	1723	150
253	Edward Simmons	1723	235
254	Saml. Westbrook	1723	150
254	Thomas Drake	1723	200
255	Same	1723	150
255	Joshua Joyner	1723	275
256	James Turner	1723	245
256	Wm. Rainey	1723	50
257	Chaplin Williams	1723	190
257	Wm. Thomas	1723	290
258	John Sutar	1723	65
258	John Drew	1723	530
258	John Poythres	1723	200
259	William Thomas	1723	130
259	John Branch	1723	100
260	Wm. Johnson	1723	165
260	Joseph Godwin	1723	100
261	Wm. Deloach	1723	350
261	George Jordan	1723	100
262	William Browne	1723	115

262	Wm. Batte	1723	150
263	Edward Simmons	1723	120
263	Wm. Scarbrow	1723	125
263	George Wythe	1723	115
316	Richard Hill	1723	200
317	Robert Ellis	1723	125
317	Elizabeth Urvin	1723	420
318	George Williams	1723	300
319	Hugh Lee	1723	325
319	John Newton	1723	75
320	Edward Wyatt	1723	200
320	Robert Booth	1723	320
321	William Gray	1723	130

MIDDLESEX COUNTY. .

Book No. 6.

Page	Name	Date	No. acres
92	Martha Ludford	1672	300
92	Rich. Whittaker	1669	158
277	Thos. Tugwell	1669	210
328	Richard Parrott	1669	158
415	Wm. Daniell	1672	115
428	Sr. Wm. Skipworth, Knt.	1672	400
448	Lt. Wm. Gordon	1672	245
512	Thomas Loe	1674	1200
511	Thomas Warwick	1674	600
518	John Lindsey	1674	700
522	John Richens and Geo. Hooper	1674	1100
522	Geo. Hooper	1674	346
524	Robert Aldin	1674	100
525	Alexander Smith	1674	110
524	John Richens	1674	400
532	George Goodloe	1674	250
537	Fra. Bridge	1674	300
585	Captn. Ralph Wormally	1675	2870

606	Robert Price	1675	450
646	Daniel Long	1678	100
646	Christ. Robinson	1678	300
647	Robert Beverley	1678	50
650	Augus. Cant	1678	750
661	Richard Robinson	1678	200
662	Robert Beverley	1678	300
663	Edwin Conway	1678	400

BOOK No. 7.

4	Maj. Robt. Beverly	1679	346
5	George Goodloe	1679	60
7	Edward Thomas	1679	1100
33	Ralph Wormeley	1680	740
112	Edwin Conway	1681	200
116	Robert Beverly	1681	300
127	Matthew Kemp	1682	450
162	James Atwood	1682	700
299	Anthony Doughting	1683	151
318	Nicholas Cocke	1683	346
355	Edward Docker	1684	210
358	Wm. Cheyney and Thomas Still	1684	245
402	John Willis	1684	1150
406	Richard Willis	1684	1340
413	Grace Lewis	1684	646
467	Richard Allon	1685	53
469	Richard Parrett, Sr.	1685	170
470	Thomas Chewning	1685	920
471	Robert Price	1685	17
471	Richard Willis	1685	300
472	Robt. Williamson	1685	389
517	Robt. Blackey	1686	23
524	John Burk	1686	191
525	Augustine Scarbrough	1686	722
581	Thomas Williams	1687	175
581	Thomas Thompson	1687	140
582	Oswald Cary	1687	460

BOOK No. 8.

BOOK No. 9.

4	Tobias Mickleburrough	1695	217
5	Same	1695	515
5	Same	1695	300
6	Bartholemew Fowler	1695	600
10	John Smith, Sr.	1695	228
34	Wm. Churchill	1696	40
36	Ralph Wormeley	1696	200
38	Same	1696	3200
111	Alex. Murry	1697	250
137	Ralph Wormeley	1697	1700
170	Same	1698	1850
184	Wm. Barby	1699	200
189	Robert George	1699	188
190	George Wortham	1699	33
206	Ralph Wormeley	1699	128
207	Alexander Murry	1699	250
239	Ralph Wormeley	1699	about 50 A.
256	Thomas Townsend	1700	190
292	Wm. Montague	1700	170
296	Edwin Thacker	1700	300
313	John Sandford	1701	150
375	Peter Montague	1701	1000
386	John Meacham	1701	150
399	Robert Terrill	1701	63
447	Valentine Mayo	1702	39
448	Henry Thacker	1702	23
449	Edwin Thacker	1702	153
450	John Sumers	1702	175
459	John Smith	1702	450
464	Edward Docker	1702	About 40 A.
498	Wm. Carter	1702	172
499	George Goodloe	1702	113
526	Henry Thacker	1703	77
528	Thomas Stapleton	1703	125
533	John Sandford	1703	150
543	Rebecca Mason	1703	120

546	David George	1703	80
547	Wm. Probert	1703	6
547	John Davis	1703	75
583	Edwin Thacker	1703	645
585	Same	1703	1100
703	John Man	1705	770

Book No. 10.

44	John Curtis	1711	31
44	Adam Curtis	1711	300
46	Captn. Harry Beverly	1711	46
89	Wm. Stanard and Chickeley Corbin Thacker	1713	385
132	John Southern	1714	18
310	Arthur Danelane	1716	41
314	John Clark	1717	18
353	Wm. Jones	1717	41

Book No. 11.

| 54 | Jacob Stiff | 1720 | 341 |

Book No. 17.

| 124 | Amy Walker | 1736 | 15 |

Book No. 21.

| 553 | James Gibson | 1743 | 40½ |

Book No. 31.

| 509 | Wm. Morgan | 1755 | 62¾ |
| 513 | Churchill Jones and John Berry | 1755 | 24A. 3R. 8Per. |

Book No. 32.

| 89 | Thomas Wood | 1753 | 50 |
| 355 | John Murray | 1754 | 112 |

Book No. 37.

| 71 | Wm. Churchill | 1767 | 495 |

BOOK No. 39.

367 Wm. Dean 1771   120

BOOK No. 41.

118 Richard Corbin 1773   192½
286 Lewis Dudley 1773   6½

COMMONWEALTH'S GRANTS OR PATENTS.

BOOK "R."

537 Jno. T. Corbin 1785   82½
BOOK No. 34.
287 Braxton Dunlavy 1796   20½

WARWICK COUNTY.

BOOK No. 1.

813 Thomas Ransha 1642   300A.
841 Henry Ballard 1642   50
903 Thomas Taylor 1642   250

BOOK No. 2.

13 Toby Smith 1644   650
25 John Rode 1645   1000
33 Zachary Cripps 1645   1050
34 Thomas Davis 1645   475
38 John Williams 1645   250
43 Edward Major 1645   300
45 Radulph Hunt 1645   300
105 John Williams 1645   150
106 John Lewis and Richard Wooton........1645   100
131 Francis Rice 1646   200
289 Thomas Maninge 1651   150

Book No. 3.

29	Capt. Nathl. Hurd	1653	533
182	Hump. Harwood	1652	2070
319	Hump. Gibbs	1654	40

Book No. 4.

24	Major Miles Carey	1655	94
24	Capt. Thos. Davis	1655	300
93	Wm. Stephens	1656	320
260	Thos. Newell	1658	700
298	Lt. Col. Miles Carey	1657	344
409	Rich. Hall	1661	100
471	Robert Pyland	1660	250

Book No. 5.

23	Rowland Beaman	1663	25
5	John Alford	1664	40
24	Robt. Chappell	1663	100
24	Rowland Beaman	1663	185
24	Saml. Chappell	1664	78
126	Evan Waters	1662	50
155	Richard Kelson	1662	250
187	Robt. Hubberd and Robt. Wolfe	1663	533
195	Richd. Hall	1664	150
262	Major Thos. Davis	1662	500
324	Humphry Gibbs	1663	40
370	John Lewis	1663	137
426	Humphrey Harwood	1663	1070
506	Col. Miles Carey	1665	92
537	John and Nathl. Edwards	1663	100
558	Richd. Dixon	1665	300
507	Col. Miles Carey	1665	103

Book No. 6.

30	Henry Filmore	1666-7	360
153	Giles Cale	1667	150
153	Same	1667	120

218	Thos. Iken	1669	1350
281	Mr. John Sanders	1669	650
304	Humphrey Harwood	1670	2644
450	Chas. Blankevile	1673	440
481	Henry Filmer	1673	360
506	Thos. Peirce	1673-4	155
593	Robt. Hubberd	1675-6	168
610	Richd. Whitaker	1676	600
611	John Wells and Emanuel Wells	1676	100
641	John Mathews	1678	2944

BOOK No. 7.

46	Robert Evarett	1680	280
47	Thos. Cheeseman	1680	550
87	Henry Cary	1681	670
103	James Cathome	1681	120
104	Henry Price	1681	97
105	Mr. Saml. Ranshaw	1681	136
105	Wm. Norwood	1681	70
106	Thos. Merry	1681	200
107	Capt. John Langhorne	1681	1990
157	John Corlew	1682	128
180	Thos. Merrey	1682	186
201	Miles Carey	1682	1590
218	Thos. Cheesman	1682	370
219	John Wells	1682	255
220	Emanuel Wells	1682	159
243	Joseph Ring	1683	250
353	Robert Read	1684	350
391	Zachariah Chappell	1684	175
403	Samuel Chappell	1684	125½
442	David Lewis	1685	217
460	Owen Davis	1685	18
461	John Powers and John Davis	1685	128
481	John Gibbs	1685	80
513	Wm. Townsend	1686	162
517	Wm. Norwood	1686	70

VIRGINIA COUNTY RECORDS89

461	Edward Mumford	1686	148
585	Alice Harlow	1686	550
678	Samuel Ranshaw	1688	132
704	Thos. Branton	1689	33
709	John Lucas	1689	300

BOOK No. 8.

33	Joseph Mumford	1690	410
144	John Nall	1691	45
168	Wm. Cole	1691	280
186	Ann, the wife of George Jackson, and Sarah Rensha	1691	220
187	Miles Cary	1691	122½
381	Seamore Powell	1694	282
74	Emanuel Wills	——	153

BOOK No. 9.

44	James Cathon	1696	53
41	Wm. Cooke	1696	29
41	Henry Royall	1696	245
42	Saml. Chappell	1696	218
44	Thos. King	1696	225
45	John Mallicot	1696	11¼
124	James Floyd	1697	74
129	Thos. King	1697	70
177	Peter Lear	1698	266
316	Mathew Goodwin	1701	134
421	Thomas King	1701	70
463	Henry Dawson	1702	363
633	Rowland Williams	1704	70
570	Stephen Burgess	1703	128
633	Charles Stuckey	1704	136
681	John Tingnall	1705	392

BOOK No. 10.

89	John Boucher	1713	144
122	Nathl. Hoggard	1713	136
193	Margery, widow of Henry Whitaker	1714	69

194	Saml. Groves	1714	132
214	Henry Hayward	1714	95
220	John Reade	1714	16

BOOK No. 12.

127	Henry Cary of Williamsburgh	1724	180

BOOK No. 13.

331	Wm. Rogers	1728	28

BOOK No. 14.

354	Wilson Cary	1731	20

BOOK No. 15.

124	Saml. Brown	1733	42

BOOK No. 17.

321	Wm. Haughton	1737	27

BOOK No. 34.

203	Thos. Whitby	1757	44

BOOK No. 42.

745	Anne and John Smith	1774	94

PRINCE EDWARD COUNTY.

BOOK No. 32.

612	George Moore	1755	1128
653	Wm. Watson	1755	719
672	Richard Woodson	1756	1629

BOOK No. 33.

426	John Gaulding	1758	400
451	Patk. Shallds	1758	400
533	Jas. Stuart	1758	113
570	Robert Williamson	1759	305

806	Philemon Holcomb	1760	200
806	John Porter	1760	280
807	Zacharias Fenn	1760	125
835	Thomas Lee	1760	134
836	James Brown	1760	400
837	John Morton	1760	400
839	Wm. Campbell	1760	400
904	Joel Watkins	1760	89
1004	John Morton	1761	200
1004	Rial Bowman and John S. Bowman	1761	277
1005	Rial Bowman and John S. Bowman	1761	254

BOOK No. 34.

573	Saml. Goode	1760	400
786	Abraham Nabors	1761	315
797	Henry Dawson	1761	400
930	John Biggers	1761	800
931	James Senter	1761	400
932	Saml. Wallace	1761	400
1003	Saml. Wallace	1762	295
1007	Henry Dyks	1762	188

BOOK No. 35.

23	Wm. Holt	1762	400
122	Joseph Ashur	1763	268
192	John Biggers	1763	400
194	John Bostick	1763	400
198	John Martin	1763	234
460	Andrew Porter	1763	400

BOOK No. 36.

600	Richard Burks	1764	77
622	Wm. Griffen	1764	220
751	John Jackson	1765	78
822	Andrew Porter	1765	800
822	Thomas Owen, Excr.	1765	400
1031	Peter Coffee	1767	400

Book No. 37.

95	Saml. Mathis	1767	400
118	Saml. Sherwin	1767	400

Book No. 38.

485	Luke Hark	1768	173
602	John Smith	1769	222
646	Andrew Baker	1769	262
701	James Allen	1769	36
743	Wm. Hall	1769	400

Book No. 39.

93	Thomas Crafford	1770	154
95	John Fisher	1770	800
97	Same	1770	400
138	Wm. Maxey	1770	391
358	John Clarke	1771	384
401	Jacob McGehee	1771	360
405	Richd. Thomason	1771	267

Book No. 40.

612	Wm. Thurman	1771	60
633	Saml. Whitworth	1771	200
683	Alex. Legrand	1772	150
698	Bracket Owen	1772	400
855	Manesseth McFela	1772	204
859	Manesseth McFela	1772	188

Book No. 41.

299	Mark Andrews	1773	145
410	Chas. Smith	1773	400

Book No. 42.

593	Manesseth McFela	1774	217
624	James Fears	1774	129
634	James Farley	1774	418
635	James Farley	1774	345
797	Thos. Green	1774	12¼

801	Wm. Watt	1774	20
818	Stephen Pettus	1774	94
855	Pryce B. Pannell	1774	236
856	John Brown	1774	1200

BOOK A.

165	Robert Good	1779	340
166	Saml. Morton	1779	44
467	Wm. Thurman	1780	209
510	Robert Clopton	1780	400
546	Jno. Le Neave and Wm. Booker	1780	338
654	Peter Johnston	1780	246
674	Peter Johnston	1780	400

BOOK B.

200	Arnold Tommerson	1779	19
369	Wm. Thurman	1780	181
388	Wm. Jackson	1780	323
400	John Holloway	1780	250

BOOK C.

56	Arthur Jameson	1781	70
62	Peter Legrand	1781	182
66	John Moraine	1781	413
204	Saml. Wallace	1781	93
216	Ezekiel Kendrick	1781	112
362	Andrew Dunn	1781	183
436	Chas. Patteson	1781	68

BOOK D.

126	Wm. Black	1780	151
336	Henry Young	1780	263
398	George Moore	1781	325
508	Jordan Anderson	1781	63½
520	John Fielder	1781	43
621	Wm. Hencock	1781	400
693	John Arnold	1781	183
710	Ambrose Hinge	1781	167

772 Bryan McDearmose 1781   300

BOOK E.

1   Charles Lovell 1775   211
196 John Watson 1780   165
924 Charles Smith 1781   202

BOOK F.

143 Peter Legrand 1782   862

BOOK G.

185 Thos. Holt 1782   211
288 Mordecai Hill 1782   332
123 Nathaniel Venable 1782   44

BOOK H.

63 Robert Peak 1783   304

BOOK I.

2   Peter Legrand 1783   128

BOOK No. 8.

605 Robt. Bowman 1787   150

BOOK No. 16.

38 Furgus Mann 1788   400

BOOK No. 20.

320 Robert Jennings 1789   250

BOOK No. 22.

159 Wm. Swinney 1790   300
699 Wm. Wooton 1791   300

BOOK No. 23.

156 Abraham Chandler 1790   92
158 Wm. Swinney 1790   133½

Book No. 26.

113	Wm. Coffee	1792	396
114	Philip Mathews	1792	301
705	John Sweeny	1792	168½

Book No. 27.

| 393 | Davis Hill | 1792 | 116 |

Book No. 28.

140	William Tyree	1792	237
141	Same	1792	22½
142	Same	1792	88
680	Richard Bibb and John Clarke, Jr	1793	152

Book No. 30.

57	Wm. Wraxton	1793	109½
409	John Thurman	1794	100
425	Robert Kelso	1794	280
426	Wm. Sweney	1794	20

Book No. 31.

18	Wm. Tyree	1793	250
20	Daniel Tyree	1793	307
27	Wm. Fore	1793	20

Book No. 32.

56	Wm. Walker	1794	95½
120	Saml. Cunningham	1794	59½
341	Dick Holland	1795	65

Book No. 34.

236	Jas. Dickinson	1796	145
498	Chas. Patterson	1796	102
576	Wm. Sweeney	1796	462
686	Saml. Watkins	1796	180

Book No. 35.

| 331 | Peter Patterson | 1796 | 185 |

Book No. 37.

170	Wm. Sweeny	1797	79
232	Stephen Bell	1797	16¾

Book No. 39.

48	Wm. Bennitt	1796	31½
189	Saml. Morrison	1797	332
485	Danl. S. Tucker	1797	98

Book No. 40.

135	Thos. Robinson	1798	290

Book No. 41.

149	Robert Kelsoe	1799	422

Book No. 42.

597	John Botewright	1779	66½

PATRICK COUNTY.

(Cont. from page 25)

Book No. 38.

323	James Turner	1798	400
367	Wm. Scott	1798	200
371	Benj. Hancock	1798	75
372	Geo. Carter	1798	145
566	Geo. Penn	1799	3156

Book No. 39.

40	Haman Critz, Jr.	1796	96
43	Jesse Com	1796	86
54	Wm. Hamlett, Jr.	1796	120
90	Terry Hughes	1796	83
272	Jas. Perkins, Saml. Blagge, Gardener L. Chandler and Wm. Coleman	1797	65,000

VIRGINIA COUNTY RECORDS 99

295 James Harriss 1799 60
299 John Walters 1799 105
450 Paul McMillin 1799 70

BOOK No. 43.

62 Geo. Yates 1799 59
63 Saml. Harris 1799 51
64 John Yates 1799 65
66 Stephen Jones 1799 100
68 John Hall 1799 145

CAROLINE COUNTY MARRIAGE BONDS.

Cont'd. from Vol. VI, page 248.

Aug. 9, 1792. John Fletcher and Flower Seizer.
June 14, 1796. John Farish and Ann Rogers.
Sept. 10, 1796. John Farmer and Betsy Wright.
Feb. 1, 1787. Edmund Gatewood and Judith Gatewood.
Dec. 27, 1787. Richard Gatewood and Elizabeth Bowcock.
Spilsby Gregor and Caroline Nuse.
Reuben Gaunt and Sally Sullenger.
Chas. Gervis and Sarah Cissell.
—— 1790. Edmund Gaines and Sukey Broaddus.
Feb. 23, 1792. John Gayle and Betsy Pitts.
Sept. 20, 1793. Leonard Gatewood and Clary Gatewood.
Jan. 7, 1794. Wm. Gadberry and Mary Barlow.
Oct. 10, 1793. Wm. Garnett and Lucy Garnett.
Jan. 12, 1796. Joseph Graves and Rachel Hay.
Nov. 10, 1797. Wm. Gayle and Lucy Dilliard.
Sept. 19, 1799. James Gray and Sally Merritt.
Dec. 8, 1786. John Hall and Frances Wright.
Wm. Hudson and Mary Guilmore.
Nov. 6, 1790. James Hughes and Sarah Seizer.
John Hopkins and Mary Anne Luck.
George Henedge and Sally Buckner.
Jan. 2, 1792. Thos. Haynes and Hannah Wright.

Jan.	7, 1792.	James Houston and Molly Page.
May	28, 1792.	Benj. Hall and Elizabeth Hartgrove.
Dec.	26, 1793.	—— Hodgins and Nancy Johnston.
Jan.	10, 1795.	Benj. Hurt and Frances Richeson.
Oct.	5, 1794.	Wm. Hudson and Frances Holloway.
Apr.	3, 1795.	Wm. Hutcheson and Milly Dillard.
Dec.	14, 1797.	Robert Hill and Phoebe Royster.
Sept.	20, 1798.	James Harris and Nancy Rains.
Mar.	15, 1798.	Epaphroditus Howle and Mary Jones.
Feb.	22, 1799.	Blocksom Howard and Rosy Samuel.
Jan.	14, 1799.	John Hopkins and Eliza Vawter.
Dec.	11, 1799.	Bennett Hutcheson and Juane Alsop.
Sept.	7, 1786.	Francis Charles Lewis Irish and Ancy Susannah Pierce.
Jan.	2, 1790.	Asa Ireland and Emland Toombs.
Sept.	7, 1786.	Littleton Jeter and Jane Alsop.
Sept.	7, 1786.	Horatio Jeter and Elizabeth Rolands.
Mar.	6, 1791.	Thomas Johnston and Milicent Hargrove.
Jan.	2, 1790.	Fauntley Johnston and Sarah Farish.
Apr.	18, 1792.	Johnathon Jones and Milly Coleman.
Nov.	6, 1793.	Washington Jones and Fanny Kidd.
May	22, 1796.	Lee Jones and Caty Blaxton.
Nov.	20, 1796.	Robert Jones and Elizabeth Wright.
Dec.	6, 1798.	John Jones and Nancy Dew.
Oct.	12, 1797.	Elijah Jeter and Rebecca Martin.
Nov.	16, 1799.	Richard Johnston and Eliza Tribble.
Jan.	12, 1792.	George Kelly and Caty Baley.
——	1792.	Edmund Kidd and Sally Jones.
Jan.	23, 1792.	Garrett Keeton and Nancy McDonald.
Nov.	15, 1797.	Joel Kidd and Sally Saunders.
		Lee Lewis and Caty Covington.
Sept.	15, 1787.	Benj. Long and Ann Beray.
Dec.	18, 1788.	James Laughlin and Sarah Coleman.
Dec.	21, 1786.	Andrew Monroe and Sarah Roberts.
Oct.	24, 1787.	James Maylain and Betty Dismukes.
		Wm. Marshall and Dorothy Griffin.
		George Marshall and Sally Saunders.

Benj. Murrah and Molly Carter.
Obediah Martin and Ann Turner.
Wm. Murrah and Elizabeth Alsop.
Nov. 27, 1788. James Mason and Fanny Chewning.
Sept. 18, 1790. Wm. Molin and Margaret Tinsley.
Thomas McKee and Ellis Carnall.
July 9, 1790. Larkin Miller and Frances Wright.
Jan. 2, 1791. Wm. Miller and Mary Durrett.
John Morgan and Eleanor McDonald.
Henry Mayfield and Milly Davy.
Dec. 20, 1792. Wm. Miller and Nanny Jeter.
Feb. 27, 1792. James Merrett and Lucy Page.
Apr. 23, 1793. Frederick Moore and Jane Russell.
Nov. 23, 1793. John McGraw and Mary Burks.
Dec. 13, 1794. Henry Motley and Ann Segar.
Nov. 13, 1794. Edwin Motley and Elizabeth Kidd.
Nov. 5, 1794. James Martin and Ann Houston.
Sept. 5, 1794. Wm. Martin and Caty Hargrove.
May 7, 1796. Sinion Morgan and Sarah Clayton.
Feb. 2, 1797. Willis Mason and Sally Kelly.
Dec. 14, 1798. Joel Mason and Jenny Kelly.
Dec. 22, 1797. Hickman Mitchell and Letty Wright.
Nov. 18, 1798. Wm. Martin and Letty Turner.
Oct. 24, 1798. Younger Martin and Betty Bowler.
May 10, 1798. Sinion Morgan and Polly Hutson.
Jan. 1, 1798. Wm. Mullin and Nancy Chenault.
Feb. 21, 1799. Richard Mahon and Eliza Gardner.
Sept. 19, 1799. Harrison Monday and Patsy Sneed.
Sept. 8, 1790. Gray Nutgrass and Edna Pugh.
Alexander Noell and Sarah Ayres.
Nov. 23, 1793. Samuel Noell and Elizabeth Timberlake.
Mar. 6, 1794. Gilbert Nokes and Caty Tignor.
Mar. 9, 1798. James Noell and Judith Bowie.
Nov. 24, 1798. John Norment and Sally Gunnell.
Oct. 27, 1798. Nathaniel E. Norment and Amelia Bridges.
John Oliphant and Fanny Long.
Oct. 24, 1793. Thomas Oliver and Mary Ann Berry.

Oct.	5, 1797.	Thomas Oliver and Lucy Eastin.
May	28, 1786.	Daniel Powers and Elizabeth Lambeth.
Dec.	21, 1786.	Reuben Pembroke and Betty Croucher.
Dec.	16, 1786.	John Page and Rebecca Crutchfield.
——	1788.	Wm. Pitts and Sally Ingram.
		Coleman Pitts and Sally Graves.
		John Phillipe and Elizabeth Emmerson.
Dec.	11, 1790.	Richard Pope and Jenny Collin.
Dec.	5, 1788.	Thomas Fayne and Fanny Fortune.
		Moses Pruett and Frances Elington.
Aug.	9, 1792.	John Parish and Polly Hewlett.
		Joseph Pitts and Sally Daniel.
Jan.	3, 1794.	John Pattee and Sally Daniel.
Nov.	23, 1793.	Levi Pitts and Elizabeth Taylor.
Dec.	4, 1794.	John Page and Sally White.
Dec.	20, 1795.	Elijah Pruett and Elizabeth Williams.
Oct.	20, 1795.	Joseph E. Payne and Peggy Pruett.
Sept.	9, 1796.	Frederick Pilcher and Margaret Alsop.
May	23, 1797.	Moses Pruett and Amy Hall.
Aug.	1, 1798.	Uriah Pruett and Alice Credle.
May	15, 1797.	Wm. Page and Peggy Vaughn.
Sept.	13, 1799.	Wm. Poltney and Betsy Vaughn.
Feb.	3, 1798.	Coleman Pitts and Lily Vaughn.
		Nehemiah Rozel and Ann Goodloe.
Nov.	3, 1786.	Robert Rennolds and Dolly Robinson.
June	19, 1788.	Hugh Roy and Elizabeth Marshall.
		Reuben Roeve and Sukey Wright.
Nov.	27, 1788.	Wm. Rollins and Sally Brame.
		George Robinson and Elizabeth Dishman.
		Thomas Royston and Susannah Hollaway.
		John Reynolds and Molly Pemberton.
Nov.	15, 1793.	Jacob Rennolds and Martha Burrus.
Dec.	25, 1794.	Thomas Rennolds and Lucy Carter.
Nov.	18, 1796.	John Robinson and Elizabeth Houston.
——	1796.	David Robinson and Margaret Huston.
Sept.	29, 1797.	Turner Red and Nancy Floyd.
Jan.	10, 1799.	Giles Rains and Dorothy Austin.

July	20, 1786.	James Smith and Sally Waters.
Mar.	8, 1787.	Richard Sampson and Nancy Stevens.
Nov.	25, 1787.	Jesse Slaughter and Lucy Thornton Slaughter.
Dec.	27, 1787.	John Scott and Patty Woolfork.
Apr.	5, 1788.	Thomas Shirley and Molly Yates.
Sept.	8, 1790.	James Sampson and Molly Stevens.
June	20, 1790.	Oliver Sutton and Elizabeth Douglass.
Jan.	2, 1790.	Alex. Stuart and Lucy Aylett.
		John Ship and Lucy Farish.
Dec.	20, 1792.	George Southworth and Molly Gleason.
Oct.	29, 1792.	John Scanland and Ruth Taylor.
Nov.	27, 1794.	Robert Sale and Anne Broaddus.
July	18, 1794.	James Scanland and Tabitha Jones.

NORFOLK MARRIAGE BONDS.

Jan.	7, 1797.	Peter Gryndl and Mrs. Elenor Cutler.
Jan.	12, 1797.	John Burket and Mrs. Abby Foltz.
Jan.	16, 1797.	Patrick Ryan and Catherine Lee.
Jan.	20, 1797.	Joseph Meissen and Keziah Spence.
Jan.	23, 1797.	John Barns and Mrs. Sarah Bruer, widow of John Bruer.
Jan.	25, 1797.	Leven Dorsey and Elizabeth Taylor.
Feb.	—	John Reynolds and Hannah Faulder.
Feb.	2, 1797.	James Ker and Pemelee Ann Goulding.
Feb.	6, 1797.	John Fulin and Sarah Wood.
Feb.	11, 1797.	Stephen Price and Margaret Sly.
Feb.	17, 1797.	Christopher Coffin and Nancy Bridgers.
Feb.	18, 1797.	John Godinicus Brown and Mrs. Catherine Driscoll.
Mch.	25, 1797.	Edward Moseley and Jennett Cocke.
Apr.	1, 1797.	Charles Ratliff and Delphe Sullivan.
Apr.	11, 1797.	Chudleigh Southwick and Mrs. Ann Naman.
Apr.	20, 1797.	Barney Corbey and Jane Long.

Apr. 26, 1797.	Andrew Leckie and Mary Brockenbrough.
Apr. 28, 1797.	Francis Hall and Gilley Cooper.
May 4, 1797.	Isaac Avery and Mary West.
May 13, 1797.	Alex. Deal and Isabella Johnson.
May 29, 1797.	Samuel S. Leffingwell and Louisa Whitfield.
June 1, 1797.	William Consolvo and Sally Wright.
June 5, 1797.	James Allen and Elizabeth Shelton.
June 5, 1797.	Simeon Peck and Mrs. Lydia Ross.
June 21, 1797.	Joseph Brown and Margaret Humphreys.
June 22, 1797.	George Lake and Joanna Syllivan.
July 8, 1797.	John Dougherty and Mrs. Elenor Regan.
July 8, 1797.	Job Gaskings and Annis Broughton.
July 13, 1797.	Johnson Mallory and Ann Boush.
July 22, 1797.	Walter Dorsett and Mrs. Isabella Mercer.
July 29, 1797.	James Goodwin and Mrs. Hannah Wolland.
Aug. 7, 1797.	Reuben Munn and Mrs. Ester Harris.
Aug. 24, 1797.	John Nimmo and Anne Archdeacon.
Aug. 29, 1797.	Richard McGrath and Mary Scott.
Sept. 6, 1797.	Richard Payn and Nancy Burkett.
Sept. 8, 1797.	John Havan and Mary Munroe.
Sept. 9, 1797.	Alex. McDannell and Mrs. Peggy Fitzpatrick.
Oct. 8, 1797.	John Dunn and Polly Billups.
Oct. 9, 1797.	Michael Mann and Mrs. Rebecca Lee.
Nov. 1, 1797.	Benjamin Pollard and Mrs. Caroline H. Norton.
Nov. 4, 1797.	Ebenezer Thomas and Maria Patterson.
Nov. 10, 1797.	Henry B. Fitzgerald and Ann Douglas.
Nov. 10, 1797.	John Gray and Nancy Coates.
Nov. 11, 1797.	Henry Sample and Dinah Bevans.
Nov. 15, 1797.	Hance Hanson and Mrs. Jennet Connelly.
Nov. 15, 1797.	Thomas Traill and Jenny Gibson.
Dec. 12, 1797	John Brown and Elizabeth Hutchings.
July 8, 1797.	Job Gaskings and Annie Broughton.
July 13, 1797.	Johnson Mallory and Ann Boush.

July 22, 1797.   Walter Dorsett and Mrs. Isabella Mercer.
July 29, 1797.   James Goodwin and Mrs. Hannah Wolland.
Aug.   7, 1797.   Reuben Munn and Mrs. Ester Harris.
Aug. 24, 1797.   John Nimmo and Anne Archdeacon.
Aug. 29, 1797.   Richard McGrath and Mary Scott.
Sept. 6, 1797.   Richard Payn and Nancy Burkett.
Sept. 8, 1797.   John Havan and Mary Munroe.
Sept. 9, 1797.   Alexander McDannell and Mrs. Peggy Fitzpatrick.
Oct.   8, 1797.   John Dunn and Polly Billups.
Oct.   9, 1797.   Michael Mann and Mrs. Rebecca Lee.
Nov.   1, 1797.   Benjamin Pollard and Mrs. Caroline H. Norton.
Nov.   4, 1797.   Ebenezer Thomas and Maria Patterson.
Nov. 10, 1797.   Henry B. Fitzgerald and Ann Douglas.
Nov. 10, 1797.   John Gray and Nancy Coates.
Nov. 11, 1797.   Henry Sample and Dinah Bevans.
Nov. 15, 1797.   Hance Hanson and Mrs. Jennet Conelly.
Nov. 15, 1797.   Thomas Traill and Jenny Gibson.
Dec. 12, 1797.   John Brown and Elizabeth Hutchings.
Jan. 23, 1798.   Richard Hurst and Ailcey Lattemer.
Jan. 27, 1798.   Thomas Smoot and Mrs. Elizabeth Hagg.
Jan. 27, 1798.   Francis Kerr McNamara and Mrs. Elizabeth Haskings.
Jan. 29, 1797.   Jacob Grigg and Mary Ann Littledike.
Feb.   5, 1798.   John Cowden and Mrs. Nancy Wallace.
Feb. 13, 1798.   Walter Herron and Ann Plume.
Feb. 15, 1798.   Joshua Brown and Mima Simkins.
Feb. 24, 1798.   James Ward and Mrs. Elizabeth Grogg.
Feb. 27, 1798.   Lewis Wilmans and Mrs. Sally Young.
Feb. 28, 1798.   Noah Prichard and Mrs. Sarah Telfair.
Mch.   2, 1798.   Wm. De Calbiac and Mary Desbois Boiffulant.
Mch. 15, 1798.   Peter Wm. Brown and Mary Pembleton.
Mch. 22, 1798.   Christopher Lewis and Mrs. Peggy Price.
Mch. 24, 1798.   Isaac Bignall and Harriot West.

Apr.	9, 1798.	James Span and Keziah Lewelling.
Apr.	11, 1798.	Thomas Moran and Susanna Hoggard.
Apr.	11, 1798.	Lem Langley and Mrs. Elizabeth Pearce.
Apr.	24, 1798.	Francis Rice and Mrs. Elizabeth Wallace.
May	3, 1798.	Robert F. Storey and Lucy Winston.
May	7, 1798.	James Spinks and Sarah Robertson.
May	12, 1798.	William Cooper and Maria Warren.
May	23, 1798.	Thomas Boush and Elizabeth Lewelling.
May	24, 1798.	Vincent Cadore and Mrs. Mary Autresseau.
June	4, 1798.	Edward Digges and Mrs. Susanna Wood.
June,	6, 1798.	Joel McDowel and Elizabeth Hacket.
June	9, 1798.	John Camp and Mrs. Ann Peters.
June	14, 1798.	David Black and Mrs. Elizabeth Stetson.
June	21, 1798.	Samuel Higgins and Catharine Cruise.
July	5, 1798.	Richard Shaw and Peggy Kennedy.
July	13, 1798.	Mathias Lukens and Ann Rose.
July	18, 1798.	Thomas Drury and Priscilla Garrison.
Aug.	1, 1798.	Henry Pallett and Susannah Carey.
Aug.	13, 1798.	John Grimes and Mrs. Polly Smith.
Aug.	14, 1798.	Captain Robert Hatton and Sarah Wilson.
Aug.	16, 1798.	Levy Jackson and Ann Braywill.
Aug.	22, 1798.	James Carline and Margaret Croutch.
Aug.	27, 1798.	Robert Reeves and Mrs. Ann Blanchard.
Sept.	10, 1798.	Eutrope Berauld and Bernardine Beon.
Oct.	3, 1798.	John Rourk and Mrs. Mary Ritter.
Oct.	9, 1798.	Ephraim Kempton and Mrs. Eliza Carter.
Oct.	19, 1798.	Flamstead Wake and Mrs. Manning.
Nov.	10, 1798.	William Jones and Nancy Barret.
Nov.	20, 1798.	John Davis and Mrs. Alice Campbell.
Nov.	21, 1798.	Michael Miler and Anne Abbot.
Nov.	24, 1798.	Francis Marie Pegeon and Mrs. Euphrosine Sumoravul Monier.
Dec.	6, 1798.	Captain Charles Mahon and Maria Lownds.
Dec.	19, 1798.	Benjamin Blundell and Ann Gordon.
Dec.	22, 1798.	James Kilgrow and Sally Stockley.

Jan.	5, 1799.	Ebenezer Moulton and Mrs. Mary Mc-Grath.
Jan.	5, 1799.	Jesse Lambert and Sally Newton.
Feb.	7, 1799.	Robert Ellitt and Elizabeth Sly.
Mar.	13, 1799.	Daniel Black and Mrs. Anne Harrison.
Mar.	18, 1799.	Egbert Everts and Elizabeth McGarvey.
Mar.	26, 1799.	William Campbell and Ann S. Dudley.
Apr.	11, 1799.	James Turnbull and Ann Armstrong.
Apr.	27, 1799.	William Lake and Mrs. Ann E. Crawley.
Apr.	27, 1799.	Fredericke Hennicke and Mrs. Amey Campbell.
May	2, 1799.	James Frazier and Rose Parker.
May	10, 1799.	Wm. Joseph Allaidge and Mrs. Dorothy Reynolds.
May	11, 1799.	Joseph Smith and Mrs. Maxey Kelly.
May	15, 1799.	Peter Daley and Mrs. Elizabeth Miller.
May	21, 1799.	John Wilson and Mrs. Mary Brown.
May	22, 1799.	Richard Harris and Mrs. Margaret Jenkins.
May	22, 1799.	Daniel Tracey and Fanny Butt.
May	27, 1799.	George Patton and Mrs. Elizabeth Boyd.
May	28, 1799.	William Rey and Peggy Dolby.
June	1, 1799.	Spence Grayson and Betsy Bowler.
June	3, 1799.	Lothrop Chase and Mrs. Elizabeth Warren.
June	8, 1799.	William Presson and Mary Pear.
June	11, 1799.	Benj. Brown and Mrs. Susannah Langford.
June	28, 1799.	John Davidson and Mrs. Fanny Reid.
July	18, 1799.	Peter Eddy and Sarah Crues.
July	19, 1799.	William Chambres and Peggy Byrne.
July	27, 1799.	John Ventus and Mary Fuller.
July	30, 1799.	Martin Fisk and Elizabeth Gilbert.
Aug.	8, 1799.	William Haughton and Mrs. Aphia Wallace.
Aug.	14, 1799.	Daniel Stone and Jane Vaughan.
Aug.	20, 1799.	Nathaniel Brown and Fanny Short.
Aug.	28, 1799.	John Tofel and Nancy Williams.
Aug.	29, 1799.	Richard Fryer and Ann Dameron.
Sept.	28, 1799.	Vallentine Dun and Chloe Dozier.

Sept. 28, 1799.   Cuddy Dun and Peggy Jolliffe.
Oct.   4, 1799.   Henry Durant and Mary Saunders.
Oct.   7, 1799.   Joseph Archer and Tabitha Joines.
Oct. 16, 1799.   Alexander Wilson and Mary Cunningham.
Oct. 19, 1799.   William Moseley and Martha Whitehurst.
Oct. 23, 1799.   John Boldery and Mrs. Elizabeth Richer-
                  son.
Oct. 23, 1799.   Jesse Newcomb and Margaret Willoughby.
Oct. 31, 1799.   William Cammack and Catherine Hutch-
                  ings.
Nov. 10, 1799.   Alexander Whitehead and Nancy Moseley.
Nov. 14, 1799.   Edward W. Hussan and Hester Chesrue.
Nov. 16, 1799.   John Dejust and Mrs. Elizabeth Miller.
Nov. 16, 1799.   Joseph Fisher and Mrs. Anne Couch.
Dec. 10, 1799.   Francis Smith and Ann Marsden.
Dec. 10, 1799.   Henry Jackson and Betsy Jackson.
Dec. 11, 1799.   Joseph Sawyer and Sarah Wilder.

FAMILY HISTORY.

FITZHUGH OF FAUQUIER COUNTY.

(Contd. from Vol. VI., page 299)

Will of William Fitzhugh of Fauquier County, dated 7
February, 1813; probated 29 April, 1817. Son William
Fitzhugh to whom he confirms a deed of gift, etc. To
daughter Ann H. Thornton; to son Battaille Fitzhugh
in trust for my daughter Elizabeth Gordon, lands pur-
chased of John Gordon formerly the property of John
Hawkins, deceased. To son Edward D. Fitzhugh, to
whom is confirmed a deed of gift; to daughter Sarah
Edmonds, confirmation of former deed of gift, and to
whom is left, chariot, slaves and horses. To sons Cole
Fitzhugh, Dudley Fitzhugh, Battaille Fitzhugh and
Thomas L. Fitzhugh, lands to be equally divided; son

Thomas L. Fitzhugh to have dwelling house, residue of estate to children, Dudley, Cole, Battaille, Thomas Ludwell and Mary Catlett. Executors: Brother Thomas Fitzhugh, sons Thomas L. Fitzhugh and Battaille Fitzhugh and nephew Henry Fitzhugh, son of George Fitzhugh. (Book 6, page 234.)

Will of George Fitzhugh of Fauquier County; dated 7 April, 1818; probated 29 April, 1823. To son Henry Fitzhugh the tract of land I live on about 1100 or 1200 acres, also tract of land my said son lives on, which I purchased of the representatives of Colonel Martin Pickett; also 200 acres of a tract purchased of Mrs. Washington; also negroes and farming implements. To son George Fitzhugh, tract of land in Culpepper purchased of John T. Slaughter, also residue of tract of land which I bought of Mrs. Washington. 1000 pounds Virginia currency in trust for my daughter Ann Baylor. Confirms to Thomas Horton slaves formerly given him in full of the share of his late wife. Mentions legacy left my daughter Mary. Mentions brother Thomas Fitzhugh. Executors: sons Henry and George Fitzhugh. (Book 8, page 314.)

Will of Battaille Fitzhugh of Fauquier County; dated 20 May, 1833; probated 29 May, 1833. To brother Thomas Ludwell Fitzhugh all the estate except certain slaves which he leaves to his relative Henry Fitzhugh in trust for his relative Thomas L. Fitzhugh; to sister Sarah B. Edmonds, a negro. Executor: brother Thomas Ludwell Fitzhugh. (Book 13, page 73.)

Appraisement and inventory of the estate of George W. Fitzhugh, decd.; recorded 28 May, 1838; John Fitzhugh, administrator. (Book 15, page 390.)

Will of Sarah E. Fithugh of Fauquier County; dated 21 August, 1837; probated 23 October, 1837. To husband Thomas L. Fitzhugh, whole of the estate. (Book 15, page 412.)

Appraisement of the estate of William D. Fitzhugh, decd., recorded 24 September, 1838. Estate to be allotted the infant children of Dr. William D. Fitzhugh of Fauquier, viz.: Francis T. Fitzhugh, William T. Fitzhugh, Thomas L. T. Fitzhugh and George W. T. Fitzhugh. (Book 16, page 94.)

Division of the estate of William D. Fitzhugh, decd. One-third to his widow Martha S. Fitzhugh, the residue to be divided into five parts and one-fifth allotted to Frances T. Fitzhugh, William T. Fitzhugh, Thomas Lafayette Fitzhugh and George W. T. Fitzhugh. Dudley Fitzhugh, guardian ad litem. 30 November, 1839. (Editor's note).—One of the children of William D. Fitzhugh is spelled Frances in the second entry.

Will of Thomas Fitzhugh of Fauquier County; dated 29 March, 1842; probated 1 December, 1843. To Henry Fitzhugh, Thomas T. Withers and Berkeley Ward certain slaves in trust, and that they may have as much liberty as the law allows, etc. Leaves $3,000 to be put out at interest which he gives to be divided amongst certain slaves. Mentions nephews Henry Fitzhugh and Berkeley Ward. Executors: Henry Fitzhugh, Thomas T. Withers and Berkeley Ward. (Book 18, page 251.)

Appraisement of property of Thomas Fitzhugh of Fauquier of property in Culpepper County. (Book 18, page 411.)

Estate of William T. Fitzhugh in a|c with B. H. Shackelford, his administrator. Recorded 28 April, 1845. (Book 19, page 321.)

Will of Dudley Fitzhugh of Fauquier County; dated 27 May, 1838; probated 29 March, 1848. To wife Lucy Brooke Fitzhugh whole of the estate, and she to be executrix. (Book 21, page 103.)

Will of Giles Fitzhugh of Fauquier County; dated 9 April, 1852; probated 28 February, 1853. All his slaves to be freed; rest of the estate to niece Harriett Ward, daughter of my deceased brother Richard. No executor named. Berkeley Ward administrator of the will annexed. (Book 24, page 303.)

NOTES FROM THE ALBEMARLE RECORDS.

Will of Abraham Childres, County of Albemarle, dated 28 November, 1763; probated 11 April, 1764. To my son William Cannon Childres all the goods that he took from me when he ran away from me, I also give him one shilling and no more. To my son Abraham Childres; to my daughter Joriah Taylor; to my daughter Tabitha Dawson; to my daughter Lucretia Tucker; to my daughter Elizabeth Thomas; to my daughter Mary Ann Carter; to my wife Lucy Childres, 200 acres of land; to my son Creed Childres, the land where I now live; to my grandson, David Pryor. John Nicholas and son Creed Childres to be executors. Witnesses: William Henry, Thomas Tilman, Charles Card.

Will of John Childres, County of Albemarle; dated 2 October, 1800; probated 1 December, 1800. My son Joseph Childres and his two sons John and William Childres; my son-in-law John Ward and my daughter Judith Ward, land in Kenawha County, and after their deaths it is to go to my grandsons Joseph Ward and Seth Ward; my daughter Prudence Thomas; my son-in-law William Ball; mentions John Ward, Senior. Friends Joseph Ward, William Howard and Samuel Skelton to be executors. Witnesses: William Irwin, William Bowman, Snr., Seth Wilkinson.

Will of Peter Lyon, Senior, County of Albemarle, Parish of St. Anns; dated 4 September, 1760; probated 11 October, 1764. My wife Margaret Lyon; my son Peter Lyon; my son Nicholas Lyon; my daughter Elizabeth Bealy, wife of John Bealey. Executors: Peter Lyon, Nicholas Lyon and George Blane. Witnesses: Alexander Blane, Hannah Blane, George Bland.

Will of Samuel Jameson, County of Albemarle; 2 June,
1787; probated September Court, 1788. To my wife
Jane Jameson; my son Alexander; my son Thomas; my
son John; my youngest son Samuel and his son Wil-
liam; to my granddaughter Mary Jameson; to Hannah
Jameson, Jane Jameson and Elizabeth Jameson, daugh-
ters of Samuel Jameson and Jane McCord, daughter of
Alexander Jameson. Executors: sons Alexander and
Samuel Jameson and Robert McCollock. Witnesses:
William Norris, John Craig, David Craig.

Will of Elizabeth Ward of Albemarle County, 15 May,
1792; probated February Court, 1793. My four sons
Henry Harrison, Richard, John and Benjamin Ward;
that Henry Austin, Snr., take my four sons and keep
them until they severally arrive at the age of 18 years,
said Austin shall be my executor. Witnesses: Edward
Frincisville, George Bingham, John Wood and Elizabeth Sims.

Will of Thomas Moorman, Parish of St. Anns, County of
Albemarle, 7 April, 1787; probated 13 September, 1787.
A tract of land in Louisa County to be sold by my executors which with land in Albemarle is to go to my
wife; my son Robert Moorman to be sent to school
until he is 16 years of age; if the child my wife now
goes with be a son, then my estate to be divided between him and my son Robert, and if a daughter, she
to have an equal part of my negroes at the death of my
wife; my brother Robert and my brother Charles.
Executors: my friends Robert Moorman and William
Wash. Witnesses: John Eades, Samuel Wood, Lau-
rence Mansfield, Zach. Wood.

10 November, 1748. Deed from John Glover of Albemarle
to Bryan Dolen of same place, 400 acres in sd. county.
Samuel Glover a witness.

7 June, 1749. Deed from Samuel Glover of Albemarle to
Samuel Baker of Amelia, tract of land in Albemarle
patented by sd. Glover 20 August, 1747.

12 Feb., 1750. Deed from Samuel Glover of Albemarle to James Spencer of sd. county, 300 acres in sd. county.

21 November, 1768. Deed from Christopher Harris to Thomas Grubbs, both of Albemarle, 1 tract of land in sd. county.

11 November, 1751. Deed from Abraham Childress to William Bugg, both of Albemarle, one parcel of land in sd. county.

6 November, 1751. Deed from John Childrey, planter of Albemarle, to Francis Childrey of same place of one parcel of land.

18 March, 1752. Deed from Robert Tompson of County of Cumberland to William Childress of Albemarle, 250 acres in latter place.

10 September, 1772. Deed from Nicholas Lyons and Martha, his wife, of Parish of St. Anns, Albemarle, to John Thurmond of same place, 1 tract of land in county afsd.

10 May, 1759. Deed from Abraham Venable of County of Louisa to Elizabeth Morton, daughter of said Venable and wife of Josiah Morton of Parish of Cumberland, County of Lunenberg, 1 tract of land in Albemarle.

11 May, 1759. Deed from Bolin Clark of Bedford County to Charles Moorman of Louisa County, 400 acres in Albemarle.

14 June, 1764. Deed from Thomas Mooreman and Rachel his wife, of Trinity Parish, Louisa County to Robert Clark of Albemarle, one tract of land in latter place.

18 July, 1767. Deed from Charles Moorman of Louisa County to Henry Wood of Albemarle, 100 acres of land in latter county.

8 December, 1781. Deed from Patrick Morton of Albemarle to George Gilmore of said place, 397 acres in said county.

11 September, 1783. Deed from Achilles Mooreman of Bedford County to George Gilmer of Albemarle, 400 acres in latter county.

14 April, 1785. Deed from John Mansfield and Sarah, his wife, of Albemarle, to Samuel Mansfield, 100 acres in said county.

27 October, 1784. Deed from Thomas Moreman to Abraham Eads, both of Albemarle, 150 acres in said county.

10 January, 1788. Deed from Elizabeth Mooreman to George Gilmer, both of Albemarle, one tract of land in sd. county.

28 December, 1789. Deed from Robert Moorman and Sally, his wife, to John Scott, all of Albemarle, one parcel of land in sd. county.

27 November, 1792. P. of attorney from Robert Moorman of Albemarle, being about to remove to South Carolina, to his friends John Hudson and William Roper.

14 March, 1793. Deed from Samuel Mansfield and Martha, his wife, to Robert Mansfield, all of Albemarle, 65 acres in said county.

9 March, 1770. Deed from Joseph Poindexter of Augusta latter county.

14 April, 1789. Deed from Lovil Poindexter of Albemarle of all goods and chattels to James Epperson and Rowland Horsley.

Marriage bond of Micajah Clark to Sarah Henderson, with consent of John Henderson to his daughter's marriage, 15 January, 1789.

Marriage bond dated 12 November, 1791, of John Clark, Jnr., to Susannah Henderson, spinster.

Will of Thomas Anderson of Albemarle County; dated 25 October, 1750; probated 9 March, 1758. To son Charles 400 acres of land; son Gideon 300 acres, a part of the home plantation, remainder to be equally divided between my four youngest children, William, David, Micajah and Judah Anderson; to William Cornwell; my daughter Ann Allen; my daughter Frances Hughes; to my children Thomas Anderson, James Anderson, Susannah Williams, Elizabeth Woodson and Agnes Peak, one shilling each. Executors: sons Charles, Gid-

eon and William Anderson. Witnesses: John Gamma-
way, Jnr., John Gammaway, Snr., Roger Williams.
Inventory and appraisement of the estate of Micajah Clark,
Jnr. Appraisers: Micajah Clark, Henry Mullins and
Richard Harvie. Amount: 382 pounds 18 shillings and
8 pence. Dated 10 May, 1774.
Appraisement of the estate of Benjamin Clark, decd., 9 Nov.
1776; recorded November Court, 1776.
Lay off of dower of widow of Micajah Clark, decd., 7 April,
1788; recorded 11 April, 1788.
Will of David Anderson of Albemarle County, 3 October,
1789; probated September Court, 1791. Sons William,
Nathaniel and David, 300 acres in Hanover County;
son Richard; to granddaughters Mary Johnson Anderson and Elizabeth Anderson, four slaves and increase
which my youngest son Matthew Anderson, their
father, has after his death; daughter Ann Minor and
to her son Thomas, 4 slaves after the death of his
mother; grandson Jack Anderson, son of Thomas Anderson, 465 acres in Hanover County; my daughter
Sarah Hudson; son Edmund Anderson, land in Hanover whereon I formerly lived; son Samuel Anderson;
grandson Anderson Barret; daughters Ann Minor and
Sarah Hudson and their children; my wife Elizabeth
and my sons David and Samuel to be exors. Codicil,
9 July, 1791. Mentions daughter Sarah Hudson and
her husband Christopher Hudson and their children.
Allotment to Edmund Anderson and his wife Jane of certain negroes, being 1-3 part of the estate of William
Lewis, decd. Recorded December, 1785.
Inventory of the estate of William Clark, decd. Recorded
2 Feb., 1801.
Will of Elizabeth Anderson, St. Anns Parish, Albemarle,
1 October, 1804; probated 28 November, 1804. Sons
Edmund and Nathaniel Anderson; grandson Anderson
Barrett; grandson Samuel, son of my son Samuel An-
derson; grandson William, son of my son David;

granddaughter Polly Anderson, daughter of my son Thomas; my two daughters Ann Minor and Sarah Hudson; granddaughter Ann Hudson. Executors: son Nathaniel Anderson and Christopher Hudson, both of Albemarle, and grandson Anderson Barrett of Richmond. Witnesses: Absolom McQuerry, William Barden.

Will of William Clark, Albemarle County, 21 December, 1805; probated 7 April, 1806. Friend Jacob Oglesby and his daughter Elizabeth Oglesby to have the whole estate, and said Jacob Oglesby to be exor. Witnesses: John Gambell, Jas. Huckstipp, James Clark, Benjamin Defoe.

Will of Nathaniel Anderson of Asylum, Albemarle County, 29 April, 1811; probated 7 December, 1812. My son Nathaniel; my deceased brother Thomas Anderson; daughter Polly Mosby; daughter of my son William Anderson; mentions William Anderson's grandfather Carr's estate; daughter-in-law Elizabeth Lawrence; my wife Sarah; sons Nathaniel and William Anderson and Samuel Mosby and Christopher Hudson to be exors Witnesses: Samuel Dyer, William H. Dyer, Celia Dyer.

Whereas Jonathan Clark and others did patent on 25 May 1734 3277 acres in Goochland, now Albermarle County, and the said Jonathan Clark did depart this life and no legal division of the said land having been made under his last will and testament, his part of the said land is now in possession of John and Benjamin Clark his sons, of Drysdale parish, King and Queen County.

Conveyance from John Clark of Albemarle County to Benjamin Clark of sd. county of part of the land left them by their father Jonathan Clark, deceased, of King and Queen, by will dated 9 April 1734. Recorded in Albemarle 13 August 1752.

Conveyance date ———— 176— from John Clark and Ann his wife of the county of ———— to William Tandy of Albemarle of 410 acres in latter county, part of a

tract taken up by Jonathan Clark and others. Recorded
11 November, 1763.

Conveyance from John Clark and Mary his wife of Albemarle County to Josiah Wood of same place, 200 acres
in said county. Recorded May Court, 1769.

Conveyance 23 December, 1748, between Edwin Hickman
of St. Anns parish, Albemarle, and Thomas Graves of
St. George's parish, in Spottsylvania County, and John
and Benjamin Clark of Drysdale parish, King and
Queen County, recites that by a patent of May 25, 1734,
Joseph Smith, Edwin Hickman, Thomas Graves and
Jonathan Clark did take up 3277 acres of land in Gooch-
land, now Albemarle, and that said Hickman and
Graves do now convey to John and Benjamin Clark,
809¼ acres of said land. Recorded March Court, 1748.

Deed of partition dated 13 August, 1752, between John and
Benjamin Clark of Albemarle of 809¼ acres in Albemarle.

Conveyance from Benjamin Clark and Elizabeth his wife
of Albemarle County of 410 acres to John Fry of sd.
county. 14 Oct., 1762.

NOTES FROM PRINCE WILLIAM COUNTY
RECORDS.

Will of Thomas Simson, carpenter, of Prince William
County, dated 13 October, 1734, probated 19 February,
1734-5. My eldest son William Simson; son Baxter
Simson; son Thomas Simson; daughter Mary Woodard; daughter Ann Simson after her mother-in-law's
decease; grandchildren Thomas and Ann, children of
my daughter Mary Woodard; wife Jane Simson to be
executrix. Witnesses, Thomas Ford, John Robertson
and Mary Evans. Book C, Page 16.

Will of Martha Lillard, parish of Truro, Prince William County, dated 17 January, 1734, probated 20 February, 1734. To son Marcellus Littlejohn; to daughter Mary Littlejohn one third of my estate when she is 18 years old or marries. To daughter Sarah Lillard one third of my estate when she is 18 years old or marries; my sister Mary Bosman; Thomas Bosman to be executor. Witnesses John Harguson, Frances Coffers and John Hergford. Book C. Page 19.

Will of John Fishback of Licking Run, Prince William County, dated 11 March, 1734, probated 19, March, 1734. To wife Mary Doarturty and after her death to my son John Jacob Fishback; to son Henry Fishback; to daughter Catherine Rutter; to daughter Elizabeth Fishback; to son Harmon Fishback; to son John Phillip Fishback; to son Joseph Fishback; to son Frederick Fishback; to my cousin Jacob Fishback. Executors John Kemper and Harmon Fishback. Witnesses, George Gint, Jacob Hollzelaw, Joseph Martin and John Ruteor. Book C. Page 23.

Will of Abraham Farrow, parish of Hamilton, Prince William County, dated 18 March, 1741, probated 27 February, 1743. To son Isaac; my wife Sibell Farrow; my daughter Lidia; my son Abram; my son John; my daughter Elizabeth; my daughter Sibell; my daughter Margaret; my wife Sibell and brother William Farrow to be executors. Witnesses, John Graham, Thomas Whitledge and Daniel McClayland. Book C. Page 443.

Bond of Jane Farrow admx. of the goods of John Farrow, decd. At a Court held for Prince William, 18 July, 1735, Jane Farrow, Thomas Harrison, Jnr., and Stephen Delisle acknowledged the bond in open court. Book C. Page 53.

Inventory and appraisement of the estate of George Farrow, decd. 7 September, 1779. Book G. Page 65.

Will of John Farrow, Detingen Parish, Prince William County, dated, 2 October, 1779, probated, 3 December, 1793. Estate to my wife Elizabeth, and after her death to be equally divided between my children. Executors, Isaac Farrow, my wife Elizabeth and William Ross. Witnesses, Jessey Bryant and Ann Bryant. Book H. Page 90.

Will of Isaac Farrow of Prince William County, dated 2 December, 1803, probated 7 February, 1804. To daughter Sibby Reno and her two sons George and William Reno; son John Farrow and his children; grandson Isaac Farrow; daughter Mary Jackson and her son John Farrow Jackson; granddaughter Nancy Strother; granddaughter Susannah Botts; granddaughter Sibby Davis; granddaughter Elizabeth Carney; my two sons-in-law, Samuel Jackson and Enoch Reno to be executors. Witnesses George W. Jackson and John Coinwell. Book I, Page 19.

Will of Francis Jackson, Prince William county, dated 10 December, 1781; probaed 7 January, 1782. To grandson Billy Jackson, son and heir to my son Charles Jackson, decd.; my son Samuel Jackson; my son Francis Jackson; my daughter Ann Jackson; my daughter Janney Feilder and her husband William Feilder; my three daughters, Susannah, Constant and Elizabeth; to Jane Marlow; to daughter Susannah Jackson when she arrives at 18 years; to daughter Constant Jackson when she arrives at the same; to daughter Ann Jackson when she arrives at the same; to daughter Elizabeth Jackson when she arrives at the same. Executors, son Samuel Jackson and son-in-law William Feilder. Witnesses: John Thorn, Thomas Smith and Nathaniel Russell. Book G, Page 142.

Inventory of the estate of Richard Grubbs, decd., of Prince Williams County, 94 pounds, 16 shillings and sixpence. At a Court held 4 April, 1787. Book G, Page 361.

Indenture this 22 July, 1746, between William Farrow, Ann, his wife, and Isaac Farrow of Dettingen parish, Prince William County, to John Graham of the same place, land whereon now lives Simon Luttrell and Abraham Farrow, containing 400 acres, being part of the land granted to Captain John Lord and situated on Quantico creek on the south side of the plantation whereon Margaret Farrow now lives, and then when granted in Westmoreland County, but now in Prince William County, conveyed first by Thomas Barton of Stafford County to Abraham Farrow, father to the said William Farrow, and grandfather to said Isaac Farrow, as by deeds, etc., dated 5 April, 1728. Recorded 28 July, 1746. Deed Book I, Page 133.

Appraisement of the estate of John Farrow, decd., 8 August, 1735.

Indenture between John Morehead, parish of Hamilton, County of Prince William, planter and Mary his wife of the one part, and John Frogg of same place of the other part, 192 acres of land granted by patent from the Proprietors of the Northern Neck, bearing date 10 September, 1742.

Indenture between John Frogg of parish of Hamilton, County of Prince William, gent., to John Morehead, Snr., of aforesaid county, planter of 180 acres of land. 9 April, 1746. Deed Book I, Page 97.

NOTES FROM FAUQUIER COUNTY RECORDS.

Division of negroes belonging to the estate of Charles Thornton, decd., between Thomas Thornton, Jnr., the children of Charlotte Curtice, decd., and Lettice Thornton. Recorded 27 April, 1778.

Conveyance from Reuben Wright and Mary, his wife, of Fauquier, and James Tutt Dickerson of Culpeper County, 300 acres of land in Fauquier for 90 pounds currency. Recorded 27 April, 1778.

Mortgage of Edward Dickenson, Snr., of Fauquier, to Alexander Cunningham of Falmouth in King George County, in behalf of A. Dreghorn & Company of Glasgow, Great Britain, for 38 pounds, one slave.

Robert Ashby, guardian to Martin and Thomas Bryan Ashby, orphans of Nimrod Ashby, decd. Recorded June Court, 1764. (Order Book.)

Inventory of the estate of Captain Nimrod Ashby, decd., of Fauquier, 29 June, 1764, also of estate in Frederick County, and of land in Stafford and King George Counties.

Will of Robert Ashby of Fauquier, dated 2 June, 1790, probated 27 Feb., 1792. To son Benjamin Ashby land on Shenandoah river, where the said Benjamin now resides. Grandson William Ashby, son of Benjamin, when he arrives at the age of 21 years, a negro girl. To son Enoch Ashby during his life the land wherein I now live, and after his death to my two grandsons Robert and Alexander, sons of Enoch; to be divided by a branch known by the name of Ann Churchill Spring branch, south side to grandson Robert, remainder to grandson Alexander. Devises negroes to son Enoch, and afterwards to said Enoch's wife Sally, and then to their children. To daughter Ann Farrow, 10 pounds. Grandson Bayles Ashby; granddaughter Molly Farganson; daughter Winifred Piper; two grandsons Martin and Thomas, sons of Nimrod Ashby. Daughter Molly Athel; to son John Ashby negroes, and he to be executor, also to him one tract of land in Fauquier, adjoining George Ash and purchased of Martin Ashby, containing 100 acres. Granddaughter Lucinda Ashby to whom he directs son John to give a negro; grandson Benjamin Farrow.

Will of John Ashby of Fauquier, dated 13 January, 1812, probated 28 August, 1815. Son Samuel Ashby, half of tract of land on Horners Fork of Licking, containing by patent 800 acres, also whole tract of land 200 acres adjoining a tract of 500 acres entered in the name of John Marshall near the Kentucky River, both these tracts in Kentucky; also a lot of land in the Manor of Leeds which I purchased of Daniel Routt; also negroes. To son John Ashby half of tract lying on waters of Horners Fork of Licking in Kentucky; also lot of land in Manor of Leeds

purchased of John Adams, also negroes. To daughter
Martha Ann Withers a negro and after her mother's death,
60 pounds. To daughter Dolly Jones a negro, also loan of 2
negroes during her life and afterwards to her children. To
daughter Elizabeth Tutt, negroes, and to the three daughters above mentioned a tract of 1000 acres on North
Fork of Licking in Kentucky to be equally divided between them. To sons Nimrod and William Ashby, negroes, also a lot of land in Manor of Leeds, adjoining the
land of Nimrod Farrow. To son Thomson Ashby a lot
of land in Manor of Leeds known by the name of my
mountain plantation, also negroes. To son Turner Ashby
a lot of land on Goose Creek adjoining Thomas Adams
on the town side, also negroes. To sons Turner and Marshall Ashby after their mother's death the land I live on,
the land I purchased of John Hickman and land purchased of John Adams. (Mentions line of land purchased
by Samuel Ashby of George Adams.) To three sons Nimrod, William and Thomson, one-half of 1000 acres on
North Fork of Licking in Ky., also 1450 acres on main
branch of Licking. To beloved wife Mary Ashby, negroes,
and after her death to son Marshall, also land I live on,
the land purchased from John Adams and the land purchased from John Hickman. Wife to be extx., and sons
Samuel and Nimrod executors.

Will of Samuel Ashby of Fauquier, dated 13 January, 1816,
probated 26 February, 1816. To wife Martha, all my estate during life or widowhood, afterwards to be equally
divided among our children, viz.: Maria, Henry, Jameson,
Mary, Catherine, Clarkson, Martha and Caroline. The
land and mill purchased of Mrs. Martha Chunn to be
sold. Executors, my loving wife Martha, my brothers
Nimrod, Thomson and Turner Ashby and Peter Adams.

Oct. 12, 1815. Settlement of accounts of the guardian of
Sarah Ashby in the presence of Willoughby Ashby, her
guardian, appointed by the County Court of Shelby in
Kentucky. Recorded in Fauquier, 26 February, 1816.

Signed by Nimrod Ashby, Turner Adams, Peter Adams. Appraisement of the estate of Major Samuel Ashby in Fauquier. Recorded 23 December, 1816.

Will of Mary Ashby of Fauquier, dated 24 February, 1826; probated 23 May, 1826. To son Marshall $30 and interest in a negro. To son Nimrod for the use of his son Edwin Thomas Ashby, $150. To the children of my daughter, Dolly Jones, one-sixth part of my estate after debts are paid. My five children, Martha Withers, Nimrod Ashby, William Ashby, Elizabeth Tutt and Thomson Ashby the remainder of the estate. William Withers, husband of my daughter Martha. The four children of my daughter Martha, viz.: Elizabeth, Mary, Samuel and Martha. Son Marshall Ashby to be trustee. Executors three sons, Nimrod, William and Thomson.

Will of Nimrod Ashby of Fauquier, dated 27 January, 1829, probated 24 March, 1830.

Wife Elizabeth T. Ashby all estate during her life or widowhood, then to my ten children, viz.: Rebecca W. Ashby, Edwin T. Ashby, Albert A. Ashby, Nimrod T. Ashby, Mary Elizabeth Ashby, Ann Amanda Ashby, Jane W. Ashby, Samuel T. Ashby, Adeline E. Ashby and John Robert Ashby. Executrix wife Elizabeth.

Will of John Ashby of Fauquier, dated 27 March, 1831, probated 25 April, 1831. All my estate after payment of debts to be divided equally among my six daughters, viz.: Eliza Neale, Mary Turner Ashby, Lucy S. Ashby, Susan Ashby, Belle Ashby and Roberta Ashby. Son William having received his portion of the estate. Wife Mary Ashby. Should I have another heir, then he or she to share with the daughters. Executor John P. Phillips.

Will of John H. Ashby of Fauquier, dated 19 April, 1834, probated 28 June, 1834. Directs sale of tracts of land lying on Crooked Run in Fauquier conveyed to him by deed from John Evans and wife and Hannah Phillips and Andrew Chunn executor of

John T. Chunn; also all the undivided interest which he
has in the land belonging to the estate of Samuel Ashby,
decd., and Martha Ashby, decd. Wife Aleinda all the rest
of estate personal or mixed for her life and after her
death or remarriage to be applied to the education and
maintenance of my daughter Martha C. Ashby, or of such
child or children as may hereafter be born, if daughter
lives to the age of 21 years, the estate then to pass to her
in fee simple, but if she die, then estate to be sold and
out of proceeds wife to receive one-third part and bal-
ance to be divided between brothers and sisters of tes-
tator. Mentions sister Mary O. Grantham and brother
John J. Ashby. Wife to be extx.

Heirs of Turner Ashby, decd., in a|c with Dorothea Ashby,
as guardian. Heirs, Elizabeth T. Ashby, Mary Ashby,
Richard Ashby, Francis M. Ashby, Dorothea F. Ashby.
Recorded 23 September, 1837.

Martha Ashby was allotted division No. 4 of the estate of
Andrew Chunn, decd. Recorded 15 February, 1847.

Will of Catherine Dickinson of Stafford county, dated 28 October, 1840, probated in Fauquier 24 May, 1841. To
daughter Letitia C. Dikinson all my estate and she to be
extx.

Will of Ephraim Haws of Fauquier, dated 14 August, 1852,
probated 23 August, 1852. To wife Marium Haws whole
estate and after her death to be disposed of according to
her will or pleasure.

    NOTE. Annexed to the will is a letter of Marium Haws
to the Court asking for the appointment of her brother
John M. Lunsford as administrator with the will annexed of her deceased husband. Dated 19, August, 1852.

Appraisement of the estate of Richard B. Buckner, decd.
Recorded 28 May, 1839.

Slaves allotted from the estate of Richard B. Buckner, decd.,
to Mrs. Louisa H. Buckner, widow of the late Richard
B. Buckner, now the wife of Thomas B. Turner. Recorded 24 July, 1843.

Division of the estate of Richard B. Buckner, Esq., decd., to the widow Louisa H. Buckner, infant children of the decd., E. Ariss Buckner, Richard P. Buckner, Ella Buckner. Recorded 28 January, 1843.

Estate of Richard B. Buckner, in a|c with Louisa H. Buckner, admx. Recorded 28 January, 1843.

Marriage bond of Richard Buckner to Judith Edmonds, dated 27 Feb., 1772.

Conveyance dated 20 April, 1793, from Aylett Buckner and Judith Presley, his wife, of Fauquier, to Martin Pickett of same place for 297.15.0. currency 555¾ acres part of tract said Buckner now lives on.

Conveyance from Aylett Buckner of Fauquier to Thomas Griffin Thornton of same place for 1215.16.3. currency a tract of land whereon said Buckner now lives in Fauquier containing 694¾ acres. Recorded 13 July, 1796.

Conveyance from Aylett Buckner of Fauquier to Thornton Buckner of same place for 427.0.0. currency, 213½ acres part of same tract in Fauquier. Recorded 12 July, 1796.

2 December, 1802. Deed of gift of negroes from Aylett Buckner to John Y. Taylor.

6 Oct., 1831. Conveyance from Ariss Buckner and Lucy his wife, of Loudoun County, to their son Thomas H. Buckner, of Fairfax County, of a tract of land in Fauquier, which land the said Lucy Buckner obtained in a division from her father's estate, it being a part of a large tract which her father bought of John Lawson, all of which by reference to the Clerk's office of Prince William and Fauquier it will fully appear.

1 July, 1836. Ariss Buckner and Lucy his wife, of Loudoun County, to their son, Thomas H. Buckner of Washington County, Mississippi. Deed of gift of 393 acres in Fauquier County, which they inherited under the will of the late Bernard Hooe, Snr.

Another deed from Ariss Buckner and Lucy his wife, of Loudoun, to their son Richard B. Buckner of Fauquier, of

1444 acres in Fauquier which they inherited under the will of the late Bernard Hooe, Snr.

4 November, 1847. Lucy Buckner of Loudoun County, deed to Alfred Moss of Fairfax as trustee, to secure a loan of $2000, made to the said Lucy by Thomas R. Love and Francis L. Smith, Commissioners of the Court of Fairfax County, as will appear by bond bearing same date with this indenture, with S. Ariss Buckner as her security. The said Lucy secures the loan by deeding "all that tract of land lying in the counties of Fauquier and Prince William, known as Vant Hill and containing about 900 acres, which was conveyed by Bernard Hooe, Snr., and Margaret his wife, to Richard B. Buckner by deed dated 16 April, 1821.

16 April, 1821. Bernard Hooe, Snr., and Margaret his wife, of Prince William County, to their grandson Richard Bernard Buckner of Fauquier, three tracts of land containing 920½ acres in Prince William and Fauquier, also a tract of 121 acres in said counties and inherited by the said Bernard Hooe, Snr., from Thomas P. Hooe, Esq., decd., as by his will appears.

24 August, 1784. Francis Triplett of Leeds parish, Fauquier, to Aylett Buckner of same place, bill of sale of negroes.

Will of Elias Edmonds, Leeds parish, Fauquier, dated 30 October, 1782, probated 28 June, 1784. Legatees, wife Elizabeth; children Elias Edmonds, Ann Hubbard, Judith Buckner and Elizabeth Bruin. Executor, son Elias Edmonds.

5 Nov., 1762. Deed from Thomas Hudnall of county of Northumberland to Joseph Morehead of Fauquier, a parcel of land 123 acres lying in said county of Fauquier, the said land having been given to Thomas Hudnall by his father William Hudnall by deed of gift August, 1762.

Will of Reuben Elliott of Fauquier, dated 29 July, 1779, probated 27 November, 1780. To William Cundiff, alias William Elliott; son Reuben Elliott; son Thomas Elliott; my wife Ruth Elliott; daughters Ann Roberson, Elizabeth

Elliott, Mildred Elliott, Jemima Elliott, Molly Elliott. Executors, wife Ruth and her son William Cundiff alias Elliott and John Obanon.

Inventory of the estate of William Grubbs, decd., of Fauquier, 21.5.6., appraised by Ambrose Barnett, Samuel Steele and John Cooke. Recorded 24 October, 1774.

Will of Samuel Grigsby of Leeds parish, Fauquier, dated 11 May, 1781, probated 22 October, 1781. To wife Ann, all the estate during her widowhood; my children and the child she now goes with. Executors Henry Peyton, William Grigsby, James Grigsby.

Inventory of the estate of Captain William Grigsby, decd. 30 May, 1782.

Will of John Morehead of Fauquier, dated 22 June, 1768, probated 24 October, 1768. Daughter Hannah Johnson; son Charles Morehead; son Joseph Morhead; son John Morehead; son Alexander Morehead; son William Morehead; daughter Mary Lawrence; daughter Elizabeth Brixtraw; son Samuel Morehead. The land I live on after my wife's decease to be equally divided between my three sons Alexander, William and Presley Morehead. Executors, my three sons, Charles, Alexander and William Morehead.

Inventory of the estate of John Morehead, decd., 392.12.9. Recorded 28 November, 1768.

Will of James Reynolds of Fauquier, dated 22 Feb., 1776, probated 25 March, 1776. All of my estate to my wife Margaret Rennolds.

Will of John Grigsby of Fauquier, dated 29 December, 1788, probated 22 June, 1789. My daughter, Fanny Routt and her husband Richard Routt; my granddaughter Jane Routt; daughter Winifred; daughter Eddy; son Lewis; son Baylis; son Nathaniel. Executors, son Lewis and Richard Routt.

Will of William Hamilton of Fauquier, dated 17 August, 1784, probated 23 June, 1788. To my brother Henry Hamilton all my estate and after his death to his children; to William Barker and his wife; to my sister Rebecca Thrift and her son Hamilton Thrift; to William Waddel; to Thomas Skinker; to Thomas Keith and John Ridley. Executors, Thomas Keith and Isham Keith.

Will of Charles Morehead, parish of Leeds, Fauquier, dated 19 January, 1783, probated 30 September, 1783. Son Turner Morehead 127 acres whereon he now resides; daughter Mary Ransdell; son Charles 127 acres of land purchased from Joseph Hudnall; daughter Kerenhappeck Morehead; sons Armistead, James and Presley Morehead, 300 acres to be equally divided; daughter Elizabeth Morehead; my beloved wife Mary Morehead; to Ann Butler for extraordinary services. Exors., wife Mary, Charles Chilton and my sons, Turner and Charles. Witnesses: George Carter, William Morehead, Richard Fisher and John Cooke.

Inventory of the estate of Captain Charles Morehead, value 491.10.3. Taken 26 June, 1784.

Will of Catesby Woodford of Fauquier, dated 8 September, 1791, probated 24 September, 1792. Estate to wife Mary, and after her death to my children; my son Mark Woodford when of age. Excrs., George Buckner, Jnr., John Woodford, William Woodford, William Fitzhugh and Thomas Buckner.

Will of Samuel Morehead of Fauquier, dated 16 December, 1796; probated 26 December, 1796, and further certified 27 Jan., 1797. Daughter Sarah Jinnings; grandson Baylor Jinnings; daughter Lydia Morehead; daughter Mary Morehead; daughter Elizabeth Morehead; daughter Peggy Morehead; son Charles Morehead; son Samuel B. Morehead; if any of my last six children die before they come of age or marry, the negroes entitled to them shall fall to the support of their mother; my wife Wilmauth Morehead to be extx. and Thomas Helm and Charles Morehead exors. Witnesses: Thomas Hunniston, Isaac Eustace, Alex. Morehead, John Morehead.

Inventory of the estate of Samuel Morehead taken 5 April, 1797, value 795.13.2.

Will of John Mathews of Fauquier, schoolmaster. Dated 24 February, 1793, probated 23 July, 1793. To Mary daughter of Josiah Fishback and Ann his wife, a tract of land lying in county of Lincoln, State of Kentucky; to William, son of Col. John Blackwell of Fauquier; to Sarah Battaille Fitzhugh and Dudley Fitzhugh, children of William Fitzhugh of Prospect Hill, Fauquier; to Mary Fitzhugh, daughter of George Fitzhugh of Turkey Run in same County. Exors., Capt. John Blackwell, William Fitzhugh, George Fitzhugh.

Will of Jeremiah Moxley of Fauquier, dated 9 October, 1803, probated 27 February, 1804. To daughter Sibella Moxley the negroes left by her grandfather Morris' will; my daughter Hannah; my wife Hannah; my sons James and Solomon when they come of age. Excr. friend Sanders Morris.

Power of atty. from James Edmondson of county of Essex to Alexander Farrow of Fauquier, dated 13 February, 1764. Witnesses: Thomas Elliott, William Farrow, Ann Farrow.

Power of atty. from Alexander Farrow, parish of Hamilton, to George Bennett. 1 April, 1766.

Conveyance 30 October, 1762, from Thomas Grubbs of Fauquier to Bennett Price, of one white horse.

Conveyance 23 August, 1764, from Thomas Grubbs, of Fauquier to Bennett Price, of one bay horse.

Indenture between Col. Richard Henry Lee, county of Westmoreland and Thomas Grubbs of Fauquier, lease of farm in latter county to said Grubbs during his life and the life of his wife Sarah, and of his son Darius Grubbs. 9 April, 1764.

Indenture made this 22 March, 1764, between John Morehead of Fauquier and his son John Morehead, land where said John, Snr., now lives containing 12 acres.

Indenture made this 22 October, 1766, between Joseph Morehead of county of Halifax, and Elizabeth, his wife, and Edward West of King George County, of a parcel of land lying in Fauquier of 150 acres given said Joseph Morehead, by his father, John Morehead, by deed of gift 26 Nov., 1753, which said John Morehead bought of Henry Cafly 8 June 1726. Witnesses: Joseph Blackwell, Charles Morehead, Lettice Chilton.

Conveyance 28 July, 1764, from William Thornton and Elizabeth his wife, parish of Hanover, King George County, and Charles Morehead, parish of Hamlton, Fauquier, 148 acres in later place.

Conveyance made 22 July, 1765, between Benjamin Tyler of Prince William County and Mary his wife, widow and relict of George Foote, late of Fauquier, and Cuthbert Bullitt of said county of Prince William and as said Mary before her marriage with Benjamin Tyler was possessed under the last will and testament of her said husband George Foote, decd., of a dwelling, plantation, etc., and a pre-nuptial agreement between said Benjamin Tyler and Mary Foote dated 12 April, 1764, grants quit claim, etc., to all title, etc., etc.

Conveyance between Pearson Chapman of Charles County, Province of Maryland and Samuel Grigsby of Fauquier, lease of plantation next to where John Grigsby now dwells, to Samuel Grigsby and his son Aaron Grigsby and his daughter Susannah Grigsby. Recorded 26 March, 1770.

Conveyance between Pearson Chapman of Charles County, Province of Maryland and Samuel Grigsby of Fauquier, lease of plantation next where said Samuel now lives, to said Samuel, his wife Anne and Taliaferro Grigsby his son, 25 March, 1770.

Conveyance 21 December, 1769, between Richard Grubbs of Prince William County and Susannah his wife, and James Stuart of Fauquier, 80 acres situated in latter county patented by said Richard Grubbs, 13 July, 1727.

Conveyance from John Morehead, Snr., after his decease and that of his wife, a negro girl to his son Samuel Morehead. 8 August, 1768.

Conveyance between John Anderson and Elizabeth, his wife, of Fauquier, to Joseph Jeffries tract of land in said county. 28 Oct., 1772.

Conveyance between Joseph Morehead of Halifax County, to Charles and John Morehead of Fauquier of one negro. 25 May, 1773.

Inventory of the estate of William Morehead, decd., 128.14.0. Dated 22 June, 1812.

Conveyance between Presley Morehead of Fauquier, planter, and Betsey his wife, and Alexander Morehead of same place, and Lydia his wife, and Mary Morehead, widow, and John Morehead, decd., of the one part and James Lewis of said county, farmer, of the second part, a parcel of land in Fauquier, purchased by the late John Morehead, 27 January, 1755. Recorded 23 November, 1778.

Will of John Morehead, Snr., of Fauquier. Dated 14 June, 1819, probated 22 January, 1821. Sons John, George, Armistead, William, Charles and James; daughters Sarah Sinkler, Betsey Triplett, Susannah Triplett, Nancy Morehead, Lucy Morehead. Excrs., son George and Matthew Neale.

Will of Presley Morehead of Fauquier. Dated 2 March, 1815, probated 27 March, 1820. To Mary Ann Rixey, daughter of Samuel Rixey and Fanny, his wife; to Presley and Richard Lewis Rixey, their sons; my sons Presley and Lewis Morehead; Frances Ann Rixey, daughter of Richard and Mary Rixey; Elizabeth, daughter of Walter A. and Catherine Smith, and Lycurgus, son of said Walter A. Smith.

Vol. VII   Parts 3—4
            September—December, 1910
                    (DOUBLE NUMBER)

Virginia
County Records

PUBLISHED QUARTERLY

EDITED BY
William Armstrong Crozier, F. R. S., F. G. S. A.

Published by
The Genealogical Association
Hasbrouck Heights
New Jersey

FIVE DOLLARS A YEAR

Virginia County Records

Published Quarterly

CONTENTS

Virginia County Records

QUARTERLY MAGAZINE

VOL. VII   SEPTEMBER 1910   No. 3

INDEX TO LAND GRANTS

BRUNSWICK COUNTY.

Book No. 11.

515	John Davis, the Welchman	1726	130
515	Thos. Avent	1726	625
516	Danl. Hix	1726	137
516	Wm. Williams	1726	220
516	Wm. Ledbetter	1726	350
517	Wm. Blunt	1726	245
517	Henry Davis	1726	100
518	John Nance	1726	142
518	Ralph Jackson	1726	100
518	Rich'd Moore	1726	540
519	Geo. Wyche	1726	150
519	Thos. Jackson	1726	195
520	Same	1726	250
520	Ralph Jackson	1726	230
520	John Jackson	1726	125
521	Jas. Wyche	1726	150
521	Geo. Wyche	1726	100
522	John Scott, Jr	1726	130
522	Henry Wyche	1726	220
522	John Bradford	1726	920
523	John Scott, Jr	1726	235
524	Wm. Macklin	1726	150
525	Matt Jones	1726	200
525	Thos. Huccaby	1726	135
525	Jas. Loften	1726	325
526	Henry Cooke	1726	500
526	John Wray	1726	280
526	Howel Briggs	1726	350
527	Anthony Crocker	1726	50
527	John Lynch	1726	330
528	Henry Peebles	1726	240
528	Isaac House	1726	286
528	Rich'd Vaughan	1726	342
529	Robert Crawley	1726	422
529	Rich'd Cooke	1726	198
530	Hy. Embry	1726	162
530	Same	1726	129

BOOK No. 13.

68	Jas. Pettilto	1726	242
68	Wm. Reed	1726	369
69	Adam Sims	1726	250
70	Francis Steed	1726	440
70	Thos. Tomlinson	1726	325
111	Howel Edmonds	1727	990
112	Peter Vinsent	1727	445
112	Robt. Munford	1727	290
113	Henry Bedingfield, Jr	1727	760
113	Same	1727	870
114	John Vincent	1727	750
114	Wm. Wise	1727	280
115	Robt. Munford and Rich'd Jones	1727	465
115	Joshua Fry and Geo. Bingley	1727	970
116	James Vaughan, Jr	1727	378
116	Jarvis Winfield	1727	200
117	Robert Morgan	1727	130
118	Wm. Beaver	1727	180
159	Geo. Ezell	1727	330
172	Moses Johnson	1727	312
173	Henry Harrison	1727	268
173	Henry Brown	1727	671
174	Thos. Jones	1727	582
174	Robert Henry Dyer	1727	997
174	Francis Young	1727	300
175	Charles Lucas	1727	770
175	John Simmons	1727	680
176	Saml. Briggs	1727	386
176	Henry Briggs	1727	165
177	John Napper	1727	300
177	Amos Tims	1727	200
178	John Simmons, Jr	1727	312
178	Thos. Dickson	1727	240
179	Geo. Hagood	1727	345
179	John Avent	1727	500
180	Wm. Avent	1727	630
180	John Bedingfield	1727	586

181	Rich'd More	1727	450
181	John and Rich'd Brown	1727	230
182	Wm. Smith	1727	790
182	Chas. Kimball	1727	550
182	Thos. Eldreidge	1727	830
183	Nathl. Perry	1727	140
184	John Alexander	1727	900
184	Rich'd Lewis	1727	295
185	Wm. Davis	1727	836
185	Rich'd Ledbeter	1727	100
186	Wm. Lucas, Jr	1727	150
186	Robert Abernathy, Jr	1727	197
186	Epaph. Benton	1727	300
187	Capt. Jas. Baker	1727	1000
188	Robert Munford	1727	792
188	Wm. Hagood	1727	330
198	John Stith	1727	398
199	Henry Embry	1727	372
204	John Banister	1727	560
205	Capt. John Poythres	1727	275
205	John Letbeter	1727	318
206	Geo. Hix	1727	260
206	John Barlow	1727	195
207	John Marshall	1727	150
207	John Ray	1727	195
208	Jas. Sexton	1727	340
211	Danl. Hix	1727	355
211	Nathl. Edwards	1727	1000
304	Henry Blunt	1728	180
339	Arthur Kavenaugh	1728	100
342	Wm. Edwards	1728	640
344	Wm. Brown	1728	467
344	Wm. Brown, Jr	1728	790
347	Thos. Cocke	1728	790
349	Joshua Clark	1728	640
350	Thos. Wright Sparrow	1728	301
358	Ephraim Parrum	1728	338

360	Henry Lound Edloe	1728	406
361	Douglas Irby	1728	648
361	Joshua Nicholson	1728	181
361	Christopher Tatum	1728	200
364	Henry Harrison	1728	2810
365	Nicholas Lanier	1728	334
382	Gilbert Ivey	1728	290
391	John Humphries	1728	541
391	Charles White	1728	410
393	John Hix	1728	960
394	Wm. Simmons	1728	321
414	Drury Stith	1729	556
427	Thos. Sisson	1728	300
427	Robt. Munford	1728	1000
428	James Munford	1728	518
439	John Davis	1728	623
440	Michael Wall, Jr.	1728	290
440	Richard Carter	1728	273
441	Matthew Smart	1728	623
441	James Williams	1728	261
441	John Wall, Jr.	1728	389
443	Michael Wall	1728	760
455	Drury Stith	1728	419
453	Simon Gale	1728	500
453	Thos. Loyd	1728	574
456	Thos. Archer	1728	252
456	Thos. House	1728	214
457	Thos. Huckaby	1728	316
457	John Robertson	1728	297
457	Chas. Williamson	1728	252
459	Chas. King	1728	872
460	George Brewer, Jr.	1728	530
473	Richard Burch	1730	254
476	Benj. Harrison	1728	700
504	Wm. Byrd	1728	1550
504	Wm. Byrd	1728	379
539	Joseph Boswell	1728	345

68	John Hight	1728	470
68	John and Baxter Davis	1728	960

KING AND QUEEN COUNTY.

(Cont. from Vol. VI.)

BOOK NO. 11.

7	James Bridgforth	1719	400
8	Robt. Deschazant	1719	130
17	Harry Beverley	1719	650
18	Robert Pollard	1720	250
18	Francis Thornton and Anthony Thornton.	1720	2740
25	Larkin Chew	1720	368
50	Richard Buckner	1720	70
51	John Martin	1720	120
51	Isaac Martin	1720	340
62	John Livingston, Jr.	1721	290
67	Wm. Glover	1721	200
106	Edward Ware	1722	815
107	Joseph Gray	1722	65
134	Robert Farish	1722	775
289	Richard Buckner of Co. of Essex	1723	4500
298	William Robertson of City of Williamsburgh	1723	1500

BOOK NO. 12.

59	Wm. Daniel	1724	100
60	John Martin, Jr.	1724	190
132	Wm. Craddock	1724	1300
500	John Baylor, Jr.	1726	3360
500	Same	1726	1300
504	John Buckner of Co. of Gloucester	1726	18

BOOK NO. 13.

108	Thomas Cary, Jr., of Warwick Co.	1727	398

BOOK No. 28.

419 Joy Asque 1748   440

BOOK No. 32.

334 Wm. Watkins 1753   172
467 John Smith of Rockohock 1755   91
682 Thos. Dillard 1756   53

BOOK No. 33.

9 Wm. Smith 1756   63
126 John Newcomb 1756   169
213 Daniel Gutrey 1756   8
459 John Watkins 1758   150

BOOK No. 34.

773 Edward Spencer 1760   63½

BOOK No. 35.

294 Joseph Abbott 1763   64
446 John Brett and Benj. Pines............1763   12

BOOK No. 36.

746 James Gardiner 1765   29

BOOK No. 37.

6 Hancock Dunbar 1767   366
33 John Richards 1767   119
46 John Dixon 1767   481
48   Same 1767   493

BOOK No. 39.

305 Alex. White 1771   80

BOOK No. 40.

842 William Fleete 1772   250

COMMONWEALTH GRANTS OR PATENTS.

Book B.

55	John Lyne	1779	115
59	George Lyne	1779	204

Book H.

224	John Lyne	1783	20¾
226	Same	1783	14¾

Book K.

321	John Thompson	1784	18½
357	Benj. Trueman	1784	90½
393	Wm. Bird	1784	16½
394	Jas. Dunlop	1784	27
395	Wm. Bird	1784	51
633	Wm. Dillard	1784	76

Book M.

231	Dr. Henry Todd	1784	130
307	John Lyne	1784	2¼
321	Anthony Gardner	1784	42½
485	John Baylor	1784	206

Book P.

9	Thos. Dillard	1784	95

Book W.

564	John Kemp	1786	53¾

Book X.

557	Stephen Fields	1785	435

Book No. 7.

396	Charles Roane	1786	70

Book No. 14.

33	Wm. Crain	1787	72

VIRGINIA REVOLUTIONARY SOLDIERS.

Miller, Jno., Private, dec'd, Contl. Line., 3 years' service; Jno.
Miller, heir at law, Sept. 13, 1783.
Hughes, Jesse, Private, Contl. Line, 3 years' service.

Randolph, Jno., Private, Contl. Line, 3 years' service.
Daulton, Moses, Sergeant, Contl. Line, 3 years' service.
Turner, Francis, Private, Contl. Line. 3 years' service.
Gardner, Jno., Sergeant, Contl. Line, 3 years' service.
Brett, Jno., Private, Contl. Line, 3 years' service.
Atkinson, Wm., Private, Contl. Line, 3 years' service.
Bishaw, Jno., Private, 1st Reg. Artillery, Contl. Line, 3 years' service.
Dugmire, Jno., Private, State Line, 3 years' service.
Bell, Jas., Sergeant, 6th Va. Reg., Contl. Line, 3 years' service.
Smith, Wm., Drummer, Contl. Line, 6 years and 6 months' service.
Gentry, Wm., Private, Va. Artillery, 3 years' service.
Garner, Wm., Private, Cavalry, Contl. Line, 3 years' service.
Garner, Jno., Private, Cavalry, Contl. Line., served 2 years 8 months 16 days.
Harrison, Wm. Butler, Cornet, Contl. Line, 3 years' service.
Power, Robt., Cornet, Contl. Line, 7 years' service.
Hoofer, Jno., Private, State Line, 3 years' service.
Hobday, Wm., Private, State Line, 3 years' service.
Scott, Robt., Corporal, Contl. Line, 3 years' service.
Dunn, Jas., Private, Contl. Line, 3 years' service.
Armstrong, Jno., Private, State Line, 3 years' service.
Leftwich, Joel, Private, Contl. Line, 3 years' service.
Somers, Wm., Corporal, Contl. Line, 3 years' service.
Cook, Wm., Sergeant, Contl. Line, 3 years' service.
Parker, Warren, Sergeant, Contl. Line, 3 years' service.
Brown, Saml., Private, Contl. Line, 3 years' service.
Leitch, Jas., Corporal, Contl. Line, 3 years' service.
Osburn, Elijah, Private, Contl. Line, 3 years' service.
Bates, Jno., Private, Contl. Line, 3 years' service.
Pritchard, Jas., Private, Contl. Line, 3 years' service.
Nelson, John, Major, State Cavalry, 3 years' service.
Stevens, Wm., Lieut., Contl. Line, 3 years' service.
Carrington, Edw., Lieut.-Col., Contl. Line, 7 years' service.
Smith, Stephen, Private, State Line, 3 years' service.
Garner, Presley, Seaman, State Navy, 3 years' service.

Wood, Jesse, Private, Contl. Line, 3 years' service.
Carroll, Thos., Private, State Line, 3 years' service.
Holt, Jas., Lieut., Contl. Line, 3 years' service.
Scott, Walter, Lieut., State Line, 3 years' service.
O'Neal, Wm., Private, Contl. Line, 3 years' service.
Bishop, Joseph, Private, Contl. Line, 3 years' service.
Robertson, David, Private, Contl. Line, 3 years' service.
Hayes, Jno., Private, Contl. Line, 3 years' service.
White, Edward, Private, Contl. Line, 3 years' service.
McClannahan, Elijah, Private, Contl. Line, 3 years' service.
Cason, John, Sergeant, State Line, 3 years' service.
Cason, Wm., Private, State Line, 3 years' service.
Cason, Jas., Private, State Line, 3 years' service.
Roane, Christopher, Capt., State Line, 3 years' service.
Darnold, Aaron, Drummer, Contl. Line, 3 years' service.
Parker, Joseph, Corporal, Contl. Line, 3 years' service.
Blackwell, Thos., Captain, Contl. Line, 3 years' service.
Howard, John, Private, Contl. Line, 3 years' service.
Saunders, Rich'd, Midshipman, State Navy, 3 years' service.
Davenport, Claiborne, Private, Contl. Line, 3 years' service.
Jenkins, Rich'd, Sergeant, Contl. Line, 3 years' service.
Rose, Archibald, Sergeant, State Line, 3 years' service.
Morrison, Hugh, Sergeant, Contl. Line, 3 years' service.
Elam, Lodowich, Private, State Line, 3 years' service.
Aspewal, Jno., Private, Contl. Line, 3 years' service.
Moore, Wm., Lieut., Contl. Line, 3 years' service.
Heth, Jno., Lieut., Contl. Line, 3 years' service.
Bridgman, Hezekiah, Private, State Line, 3 years' service.
Bayley, Noah, Private, State Line, 3 years' service.
Johnston, Wm., Captain, Contl. Line, 3 years' service.
Hawley, Rawleigh, Private, Contl. Line, 3 years' service.
Peyton, Francis, Private, Contl. Line, 3 years' service.
Fitzsimmons, Nicholas, Private, Contl. Line, 3 years' service.
Kenny, Rich'd, Private, Contl. Line, 3 years' service.
Brady, Michael, Corporal, Contl. Line, 3 years' service.
Blackson, Bridax, Private, Contl. Line, 3 years' service.
Matthews, Wm., Corporal, State Line, 3 years' service.

Blackmore, Geo., Lieut., Contl. Line, 3 years' service.
Noland, Pierce, Lieut., Contl. Line, 3 years' service.
Dunn, Joshua, Private, Contl. Line, 3 years' service.
Mitchell, David, Private, Contl. Line, 3 years' service.
Boyd, Francis, Private, Contl. Line, 3 years' service.
Stephens, John, Sergeant, decd., Contl. Line, 3 years' service;
Joseph Stephens, heir at law, Oct. 9, 1783.
Carrell, Jno., Sergeant, Contl. Line, 3 years' service.
Harris, Jno., Private, Contl. Line, 3 years' service.
Hampton, Thos., Private, State Line, 3 years' service.
Smith, Wm., Lieut., Contl. Line, 3 years' service.
McQuillen, Robt., Private, Contl. Line, May, 1777, to 10 Jan.,
1782.
Walker, John, Private, Contl. Line, 3 years' service.
Durham, Jas., Private, Contl. Line, 3 years' service.
Robins, Jno., Lieut., Contl. Line, 3 years' service.
Royster, Jno., Sergeant, State Line, 3 years' service.
Robinson, Mordecai, Private, State Line, 3 years' service.
Charles, Wm., Private, State Line, 3 years' service.
Plunket, Reuben, Corporal, Contl. Line, 3 years' service.
Stith, John, Captain, Contl. Line, 3 years' service.
Jerow, Jacob, Private, State Line, 3 years' service.
Stewart, Benj., Private, Contl. Line, 7 years' service.
Grimsley, Jas., Private, Contl. Line, 3 years' service.
Kimble, Robt., Private, Contl. Line, 3 years' service.
Clark, Moses, Private, Contl. Line, 3 years' service.
Patillo, Jas., Sergeant, Contl. Line, 3 years' service.
Tyler, Wm., Private, State Line, 3 years' service.
Eppes, Rich., Sergeant, Contl. Line, 3 years' service.
Faris, Wm., Private, Contl. Line, 3 years' service.
Robinson, Green, Private, State Line, 3 years' service.
Foster, Wm., Private, Contl. Line, 3 years' service.
Eaton, Joseph, Private, Contl. Line, 3 years' service.
Singleton, Joshua, Sergeant, State Line, 3 years' service.
Davis, Sam'l., Private, Contl. Line, 3 years' service.
Jaso, Wm., Private, Contl. Line, 3 years' service.
Perryman, Dan'l., Private, Contl. Line, 3 years' service.

Mahoney, Jas., Private, Contl. Line, 3 years' service.
Foster, Geo., Private, Contl. Line, 3 years' service.
Blackwell, Sam'l., Captain, decd., State Line, 3 years' service;
    John Blackwell, heir at law, Oct. 15, 1783.
Grey, Wm., Private, Contl. Line, 3 years' service.
Martin, Jno., Private, Contl. Line, 3 years' service.
Brown, Robt., Private, State Line, 3 years' service.
Walker, Henry, Private, Contl. Line, 3 years' service.
Tunstall, Thos., Sergeant-Major, Contl. Line, 3 years' service.
Jennings, John, Sailing Master, State Navy, 3 years' service.
Walker, Jno., Private, Contl. Line, 3 years' service.
Robinett, Joseph, Private, Contl. Line, 7 years' service.
Corbett, Jno., Private, Contl. Line, 3 years' service.
Bedworth, Wm., Private, Contl. Line, 3 years' service.
Collins, Peter, Private, Contl. Line, 3 years' service.
Mason, Thos., Private, decd., State Line, 3 years' service;
    Wm. Mason, heir at law, Oct. 16, 1783.
Scott, John, Capt.-Lieut., State Line, 3 years' service.
Hoffman, Joseph, Private, State Line, 3 years' service.
Hoffman, Reuben, Private, State Line, 3 years' service.
Scott, Joseph, Jr., Capt., Contl. Line, 3 years' service.
Drake, Michael, Private, Contl. Line, 3 years' service.
Jones, Peter, Capt., Contl. Line, 3 years' service.
Walker, David, Lieut., Contl. Line., 3 years' service, ending
    16 May, 1779.
Hood, Thos., Sergeant-Major, Contl. Line, 3 years' service.
Guthery, Geo., Lieut., Contl. Line, 3 years' service.
Mechen, Dr. Wm., Surgeon, Contl. Line, 3 years' service.
Heth, Henry, Captain, Contl. Line, 3 years' service.
Pace, Wm., Private, Contl. Line, 3 years' service.
Pickett, Jno., Private, Contl. Line, 3 years service.
Moody, Wm., Private, Contl. Line, 3 years' service.
Ballance Willis, Corporal, State Line, 3 years' service.
Ballance, Henry, Sergeant, State Line, 3 years' service.
McClurg, Jas., Director of State Hospital, 6000 acres, Oct. 21,
    1783.

Harrison, Wm., alias Starke, Drummer, Contl. Line, 3 years' service.

Harris, Wm., Private, Contl. Line, 3 years' service.

Grant, Jno., Private, Contl. Line, 3 years' service.

Bentley, Jeremiah, Private, Contl. Line, 3 years' service.

Goulding, Jesse, Private, State Line, 3 years' service.

Langfitt, Thos., Private, Contl. Line, 3 years' service.

Summerson, Geo., Private, Contl. Line, 3 years' service.

Lee, Richeson, Corporal, State Line, 3 years' service.

Langfitt, Philip, Private, Contl. Line, 3 years' service.

Kent, Smith, Sergeant, Contl. Line, 3 years' service.

Lee, Richard, Private, Contl. Line, 3 years' service.

Christie, Dr. Thos., Surgeon, Contl. Line, 7 years' service.

Hogland, Evert, Corporal, Contl. Line, 3 years' service.

Hughes, Benj., Private, Contl. Line, 3 years' service.

Brown, Jas., Private, Contl. Line, 3 years' service.

Russell, Nicholas, Private, Contl. Line, 3 years' service.

Hulse, Wm., Sergeant, Contl. Line, 3 years' service.

Brown, Geo., Private, Contl. Line, 3 years' service.

Case, Wm., Private, Contl. Line, 3 years' service.

Hutcheson, Thos., Sergeant, Contl. Line, 3 years' service.

Dowell, Wm., Sergeant, Contl. Line, 3 years' service.

Mothershead, Nath'l., Sergeant, Contl. Line, 3 years' service.

Straughan, Presley, Private, decd., Contl. Line, 3 years' service; Jas. Straughan, heir at law, Oct. 27, 1783.

Cogwell, Fred'k., Private, State Line, 3 years' service; Zach. Cogwell, representative of Fred'k. Cogwell, Oct. 27, 1783.

Gay, Francis, Lieut., Contl. Line, 3 years' service.

Hudson, Rush, Corporal, Contl. Line, 3 years' service.

Pool, Baxter, Private, Contl. Line, 3 years' service.

Woodson, Tarlton, Major, Contl. Line, 3 years' service.

King, Francis, Private, State Line, 3 years' service.

Belvin, Geo., Private, Contl. Line, 3 years' service.

Belvin, Lewis, Private, Contl. Line, 3 years' service.

Tetkins, John, Private, Contl. Line, 3 years' service.

Hearn, Danl., Sergeant, Contl. Line, 3 years' service.

Pound, Wm., Corporal, State Line, 3 years' service.

Carrington, Geo., Lieut., Contl. Line, 3 years' service.

ACCOMAC COUNTY RECORDS.

(Cont. from Vol. VI.)

19 February, 1633. Deposition of Henry Bagwell, aged 43 years.

28 March, 1633. Conveyance from Captain Edmund Scarborough to John Harlow. Witnesses: Edmund Scarborough, Jr., and Liveinge Denwood.

At a Court held the —— day of April, 1634, there were present: Captain Edmund Scarborough, Mr. William Andrews, Mr. William Stone and Mr. William Burdett.

Deposition of John Major, aged 27 years, concerning an agreement between Captain Scarborough and Philip Taylor.

Deposition of Richard Wadlow, aged 24 years, concerning James Davis and John Ford.

Petition to the Court of William Roper against Henry Bagwell.

Complaint to the Court of Edward Beastweeke against Thomas Nute.

Alexander Bradburne was arrested to appear at this Court.

At a Court held the 17th day of ——. Present,: Captain Edmund Scarborough, Mr. Obedience Robins, Mr. William Stone, Mr. John Wilkins.

At this Court Richard North commenced suit against Rowland Williams.

At this Court John Wadlow of Accomac, mariner, aged 24 years, testified in the suit brought by Philip Taylor against Captain Scarborough.

Bond of Richard North to Thomas Arnold, deceased, whereby payment is to be made to the lawful executors and assigns of said Arnold as by bond appeareth under the hands of said North and William Milling, gent. Witnessed by Henry Bagwell and William Moreton.

At a Court held the 19th day of May, ——. Present: Mr.

Obedience Robins, Mr. John Howe, Mr. William Burdett, Mr. William Andrews, Mr. John Wilkins.

Suit brought by Mr. William Cotton, minister of God's word, against Thomas Allen for swearing.

Suit brought by Susan Helline, widow, against John Major for her payment and time in looking to his wife the time she did lay in childbed, and upon due examination and the oath of Agnes Williams, it is ordered that the said John Major shall pay unto Susan Helline, 18 hens within this month, and he shall pay the said Susan by September next 30 hens, and also the charges of this suit.

Agnes Williams, aged 24 years, deposes that Maudlen, the wife of John Major, did bargain with Susan Helline, widow, for help while she lay in childbed, and did promise to give her 12 hens, which hens were to be paid by Anno Domini 1632.

Suit of Philip Chapman against Henry Bagwell.

Suit of Gates Bashaw against Daniel Cugley.

Petition of William Berryman against Daniel Cugley for miscalling and striking him.

12 March, 1633. Conveyance of a black heifer from Captain Edmund Scarborough to Garrett Andrews.

At a Court held 5 July, 1634. Present: Captain William Clayborne, Esqr., Mr. Obedience Robins, Mr. William Burdett, Mr. John Howe, Mr. William Andrews, Mr. William Stone, Mr. John Wilkins.

This day was read an order from the Governor and Council dated 14 March last past, requiring that Sheriffs should be appointed in the several parts of the Colony. In conformity to which order Mr. William Stone was chosen Sheriff of these plantations of Acchawmacke for the ensuing year.

In like manner Captain William Clayborne being appointed Lieutenant for this Shire, did appoint Obedience Robins, gent., his Deputy.

At a Court held the 9th July, 1634. Present: Obedience Robins, gent.; John Howe, gent.; William Stone, gent.; William Burdett, gent.; William Andrews, gent.

Suit of William Bashawe against Mr. Robins.

Petition to the Court of Philip Chapman against Israel Hill.

Petition to the Court of Peter Fyerbrasse against John Angood.

Petition to the Court of John Angood against Mr. John How.

Deposition of William Berryman, aged 32 years.

Acknowledgement of John Littel.

Acknowledgement of Nicholas Hanwoode.

Acknowledgment of Thomas Butler.

Deposition of Edward Gaines, aged 30 years, this 7th day of July, that Captain John Stone borrowed of John Foster 6 barrels of corn.

At a Court held the 8th day of September, 1634. Present: Mr. Obedience Robins, Mr. John How, Mr. William Burdett, Mr. William Stone, Mr. William Andrews.

Petition of Edward Drew for confirmation of land granted to him the 4th of December, 1633, which was about 100 acres of land next unto Thomas Powells.

Suit of David Windley for a patent of 100 acres of land due him.

Deposition of John Fisher, aged 30 years, concerning land rented by Captain Epes and Henry Glover, the latter now deceased. Mentions James Knott, Philip Chapman and John Major as also renting same land.

Francis Millicent agrees to serve Philip Chapman 2 years' time from the 10th of January last,

Suit of Nicholas Harwood to have the lease of land renewed where he now lives, which was formerly in the possession of George Travellor, and which said Travellor bought of Roger Sanders.

RICHMOND COUNTY WILLS.

Tomlin, George, 15 December, 1705; probated 6 February, 1705. To my son George the land formerly belonging to my Uncle Taylor; my daughter Anne Tomlin; my wife

Hannah to be executrix. Witnesses: James Ingo, Sara Lilly, Henry Street.

Mackmelion, John. 14 October, 1701; probated 6 February, 1705. My eldest daughter Charity; my youngest daughter Catherine; to John Newman; to George Newman; to William Coleman; to Maxfield Brown; my wife Frances to be executrix. Witnesses: John Fennell, Henry Street.

Clarke, Robert, Parish of Farnham, 12 December, 1705; probated 6 February, 1705. My son Robert; my daughter Catherine Clarke; my son John; my son George; my son Thomas; Captain Charles Barker; my wife executrix and my son Robert executor; to William Simms. Witnesses: Charles Barber, William Simms, Amy Simms.

Cleton, William. 29 December, 1705; probated 6 March, 1705. To Alexander and Steven my younger sons; to daughter Mary Cleton; to son William; to daughters Elizabeth and Hannah Cleton; my wife to be executrix. Witnesses: William Linton, William Lendman.

Jones, Christopher. 18 October, 1705, probated 6 December, 1705. To Margaret, daughter of Elizabeth Dudley; my wife Elizabeth Jones to be executrix. Witnesses: Nicholas Smith, Elizabeth Elam.

Dodson, Charles. 11 January, 1703; probated 6 February, 1705. To son Charles; to son Thomas; to son Bartholomew Richard Dodson; to son William; to son John; to son Lambert; to daughters Anne and Elizabeth Dodson; wife Anne to be executrix.

Tayler, George. 24 June, 1706; probated 7 August, 1706. To daughter Martha Gaines; to George Gaines, youngest son of said Martha Gaines; to Daniel Gaines, eldest son of Bernard Gaines and the said Martha; to Henry Wilson; to Thomas Dickenson, the writer of this, my will; wife Susanna to be executrix. Witnesses: Robert Gorden, Elizabeth Bradley, Anna Post, Edward Jeffrey, Thomas Dickenson.

Williams, John. 27 January, 1704-5; probated 7 August, 1706.

All my estate to Stephen Fewell and his children. Witnesses: John Owen, Richard Rosser, Richard Pearle.

Austin, Henry. 8 February, 1687; probated 2 October, 1706. All my estate to my wife Anne. Witnesses: Thomas Gunston, Francis Jordan, Walter Willett.

Kenyon, John. 29 August, 1706; probated 2 October, 1706. To son Abraham; to daughter Anne; to daughter Sarah; to son John; Daniel Merrett to be executor. Witnesses: William Thornton, George Davis, Sarah Davis.

Cunstable, Margaret. 25 June, 1705; probated 6 November, 1706. To nephew John, son of Mark and Elizabeth Toon; to John, William and Mark, sons of the above named; Mark Toone, Snr., to be executor. Witnesses: Robert Nethercutt, Austin Brockenborough.

Wilson, Elias. 23 December, 1706; probated 5 February, 1706. To eldest son Elias; my wife Mary to be executrix; my brothers Henry and James Wilson to be overseers. Witnesses: Henry Seger, Anna Post, John Kelly.

Jackson, Daniel, North Farnham Parish. 13 November, 1706; probated 5 February, 1706. Sons David and Nathaniel; my three daughters Mary Settle, Sarah Gower and Anne Hutt; my son Daniel to be executor. Witnesses: Joshua Lawson, Stephen Wells, Thomas Dickenson.

Tayler, Henry Parker. 24 January, 1706-7, probated 5 February, 1706-7. To Thomas Ward; to Austin Brockenborough; servant John Simcocke to be executor. Witnesses: John Charteris, Thomas Ward, Mary Jones.

Walker, John, County of Rappahannock. 22 February, 1665; probated 14 February, 1706. Daughter Anne Walker; daughter Frances Walker; daughter Jane Walker; daughter Elizabeth Walker; daughters Sarah and Hester Walker; wife Sarah to be executrix. Codicil dated 6 July, 1668. Mentions daughter Anne and her husband John Payne. Witnesses: Joseph Chissell, Richard Fox.

Williams, Luke. 17 April, 1706; probated 5 March, 1706. Son John; friend Martin Sherman; son Henry; nephews William Frestoe and Richard and Thomas Smith; wife

Mary to be executrix. Witnesses: Richard Hinds, John Miller, Henry Jennings.

Woodyates, Thomas, of Bristol, in the Kingdom of Gt. Britain. 20 January, 1706-7; probated 5 March, 1707. To friend Job Hamon, Jr.; friend William Hamon; friend John Hamon; friend Jane Thorn; Anne Hamon; Joyce Hamon; Elizabeth Hamon; friend Job Hamon, Snr., to be executor. Witnesses: Martin Hamon, Martin Hamon, Jnr., and John Burk.

Trent, James. 5 January, 1706; probated 1 October, 1707. Daughters Elizabeth, Anne, Mary and Alice; my wife Alice; wife and John Dean to be executors. Witnesses: Giles Mathews, John Curtis, Elizabeth Deane.

Stone, William, Farnham Parish. 7 November, 1704; probated 31 January, 1707. Sons Philip and Joshua; son-in-law Robert Scolfield; grandsons Gregory and John Glascocke; wife Sarah to be executrix; daughter Elizabeth Stone; daughter Mary Farr.

Hamock, John, Planter. ————; probated 15 February, 1707. All estate to son William Hamock; Thomas Bryant to be overseer. Witnesses: Thomas Bryant, Edward Talbert, David Bennehan.

Evans, Peter. 13 June, 1706; probated 3 July, 1706. Sons Richard, Peter and John Evans; daughters Sarah and Anne Evans; wife Elizabeth to be executrix. Witnesses: Matt. Burrows, James Dowling, Thomas Dickenson.

White, Richard. 31 October, 1706; probated 7 July, 1708. Son John; daughter Hester Mills; daughter Susanna Adcock; sons Thomas and William; wife Sarah; son Thomas to be executor. Witnesses: George Murdock, John Willcocke, John Callahan.

Dew, Thomas. 23 December, 1708; probated 2 February, 1708. Wife Jean; son-in-law William Baker; daughter-in-law Elizabeth Baker; daughter Anne Dew; daughter Mary Dew; daughter Elizabeth Dew; son Thomas to be executor. Witnesses: Peter Kippas, George Habron, Andrew Dew.

Gaythins, John. 29 November, 1708; probated 2 February, 1708. My youngest son Cobbam Gaythings; sons Phillip and John; wife Anne and my eldest son Phillip to be executors. Witnesses: Edward Jones, John Buxstone.

Price, John. 11 September, 1707; probated 2 February, 1708. Cousin Edward Price; brother Edward Price; cousin John Price, son of my brother Edward. Witnesses: James Jones, Walter Francis.

Settle, Francis. 11 July, 1707; probated 12 August, 1707. Son John; son Thomas; grandson Francis, son of Francis Settle, Jnr., decd.; grandson Henry Settle, son of Henry Settle, decd.; grandson Francis Settle, son of Henry Settle, decd.; wife Mary; son Thomas, and son-in-law Thomas Williams to be executors. Witnesses: Thomas Swindley, Alex. Young, Thomas Dickenson.

HENRICO COUNTY RECORDS.

Deed of conveyance, 2 April, 1688, from William Puckett of Bristol Parish, Henrico, to Richard Kennon. Anne Puckett, the wife, relinquishing her dower.

William and Thomas Puckett, sons of the late John Puckett, decd., division of land between them, 12 October, 1688.

Indenture made this 1 August, 1688, between Francis Cater of the County of Henrico and Philip Turpin of same place, a parcel of land in said county. Martha Cater, the wife, relinquishes her dower.

Inventory of the goods, etc., of Thomas Shippey, decd., sworn to by Joseph Royall, Martin Elam, Abraham Womack and Edward Stratton, by Frances, the relict and administratrix, 12 October, 1688.

In the name of God, Amen. I, Thomas Shippey, being sick and weak of body but sound and of perfect memory, etc. All that I had by my wife I desire may be equally divided between my wife and child. I give all my lands to my dear child Frances, only my wife to have all the land lying be-

yond the run by Edward Stratton, Jnr., during her widowhood; all my cattle I give to my wife and child equally.
The original of ye above record was this day in open
court presented by Mr. James Minge as the last will
(though unsigned) of Thomas Shippey.

Mrs. Martha Stratton deposes on oath that she heard her son
Thomas Shippey upon his death bed say that he gave what
estate he had to his wife and child.

Miss Martha Stratton, the younger, declares that she heard
her brother Thomas Shippey upon his death bed say that
he gave his estate that he had to his wife and child.
Henrico Court, 12 October, 1688.

Deed of conveyance from Francis Warren of New Kent
County to Edward Maxfield of one parcel of land in the
County of Henrico. 12 October, 1688. Witnessed by
John Woodson and Edward Mosby.

An account of the debts of Charles Clay, decd., by me, Hannah
Clay, his widow, entered 12 October 1688.

A conveyanace to the Hon. William Byrd, who formerly purchased of William Giles, who married Bethaniah, the
daughter and heiress of Captain John Knowles, decd., of
two parcels of land comprising about 100 acres. Said
sale is confirmed and entered at this Court.

Deposition of Thomas Puckett, aged 32 years or thereabouts,
in which is mentioned Mary Granger, the wife of John
Granger. Rec. 12 October, 1688.

An account of Licenses for marriage as delivered by Captain
William Randolph, who grants them:

Mr. Peter Jones for a marriage with Mrs. Mary Batte.

William Chambers for a marriage with Elizabeth
Ferris.

William Withers for a marriage with Elizabeth Bull-
ington.

Samuel Trottman for a marriage with ye widow
Lewis.

Recorded at October General Court.

Indenture made between Samuel Fowler, Jnr., of Henrico and

Henry Randolph of a parcel of land in above county. 30 November, 1688. Witnessed by Thomas Cocke and Lewis Watkins.

Deed of conveyanace from William Porter to Robert Woodson, of one parcel of land in Henrico County, it being part of a greater dividend granted unto said Robert Woodson, John Woodson, Thomas East and said William Porter and Robert Clark, by Patent bearing date 28 September, 1681. Henrico Court, 1688.

Inventory of the estate of Thomas Fields presented by Edward Jones, administrator.

Inventory of the estate of William Dodd, decd., presented by Mr. James Royall. 30 November, 1688.

Deed of conveyance of one cow from Thomas Bott to Elizabeth Kent. Recorded at Court, 1688.

Deposition of Philip Turpin, aged 32 years or thereabouts, in action between Womeck and Cater. Deposition of Jane Gower, about 48 years; Martha Osborn, aged about 26 years, and Joseph Tanner, aged about 27 years, all relative to above case.

Deposition of John Watson, aged about 40 years; Francis Rowen, aged about 21 years; Charles Hill, aged about 25 years; Stephen Cocke, aged about 22 years; John Bayley, aged about 36 years, and George Pattison, aged about 46 years, in case between Baxter and Webb.

Conveyance from Edward Hatcher of Henrico, planter, to William Cox and Richard Cox, planters, of same county, 300 acres of land granted by patent to said Edward Hatcher 6 October, 1675. Recorded — October, 1688. Witnessed by Edward Tanner and William Giles.

Conveyance from Richard Hudson, son and heir of Richard Hudson, late of Roxdale, Henrico County, decd., whereas my said late father by his last will, dated 25 October, 1669, did give unto me and my two brothers, Robert and William, a plantation at Roxdale, I now convey my interest in said plantation to my brother Robert Hudson. 1

October, 1688. Mary Hudson, wife of Richard Hudson, relinquishes her dower rights.

Power of attorney from John Brodnax to Henry Randolph, dated 26 April, 1688.

VIRGINIA GENEALOGIES.

THE HUGUENOT FAMILY OF FAURE.

Of the army of William of Orange, numbering eleven thousand, which sailed from Holland, and by whose aid he obtained the Crown of England, three regiments, each containing seven hundred and fifty effective men, were Huguenots. To these were added a squadron of horse. In gratitude to these zealous and effective supporters, and in sympathy with the great multitude of their suffering brethren driven violently from their homes and natives country simply for their religion, the King invited them to make their home in his new dominions in America. A large number sought a home in Virginia and settled along the Potomac, Rappahannock and James rivers.

In the year 1700, more than five hundred emigrants, at the head of whom was the Marquis de la Muce, were landed in Virginia by four successive debarkations. (Beverley's History of Va., page 244.) They appear to have settled at different points; a portion about Jamestown, some in Norfolk county, others in Surry, and two hundred or more at a spot some twenty miles above Richmond, on the south side of James River (now in Powhatan county), where ten thousand acres of land, which had been occupied by the extinct Manakin tribe of Indians, were given to them. They were also exempt from the payment of taxes for seven years, and were allowed to support their minister in their own way.

The records relating to the emigration to Virginia in 1700 of the Huguenot refugees, are taken from the originals now deposited at the Bodleian Library, Oxford University, England. These originals consist of a vellum bound volume of MSS. endorsed:

"ORIGINAL PAPERS RELATING TO THE FRENCH PLANTA-
TION IN THE WEST INDIES."

They are undoubtedly the original documents emanating
from the Provincial Government of Virginia under Francis
Nicholson, as they bear the official signature of Dionisius
Wright, who was Secretary to the Council. We now find the
name of Faure under the following heading:

"A LIST OF THE REFUGEES WHO ARE TO RECEIVE OF
YE MILLER OF FALLING CREEK MILL ONE BUSHEL A
HEAD OF INDIAN MEALE MONTHLY AS SETTLED AT OR
ABOUT KING WILLIAMS TOWN, TO BEGIN IN FEB, 1700-1.
"FFAURE, his brother, and two sisters. . . . .4.

"ROLLE DES FRANCOIS, SUISSES, GENEVOIS, ALEMANS,
ET FLAMANS EMBARQUES DANS LE NAVIRE NOMME LE
NASSEAU POUR ALLER A LA VIRGINIE.
"PIERRE FFERRE, sa femme et un enfant.

"A LIST OF YE FRENCH REFUGEES THAT ARE SETTLED
ATT YE MANNACHIN TOWN ARE AS FOLLOWS:
In ye first Shipp
"FFAURE, his brother and sister. . . . .3."

From the above it will be seen that Pierre Faure had with
him a brother and two sisters, as well as his wife and one child.
The brother's name was undoubtedly Daniel, after whom
Pierre named one of his sons. The name of the two sisters
cannot be ascertained.

DANIEL FAURE BROTHER OF PIERRE FAURE.

From the land grants at Richmond we find that a grant
of 296 acres was given Daniel Faure the 3d day of March,
1715, the said land lying chiefly in Henrico county. (Book 10,
page 285.)

In the "Vestry Book" of King William Parish, Manniken
Town, under date of a Vestry assembled 25 August, 1718, the
"Sieur Daniel Faure is elected a vestryman." As Pierre Faure
was not granted land until 1716, and then only 107 acres, it is

almost impossible that his son Daniel should have had a large grant of 296 acres given him a year ahead of his father, and he was too young to have been elected a Vestryman in 1718. The name of a Daniel Faure is found on the list of Tithables in King William Parish from the year 1717 to 1736. During the later years it was more than likely Daniel, the son of Peter, is meant. While no will of Daniel Faure can be found, it is extremely probable he was a brother of Pierre, Snr., and that Daniel, the son of Pierre, was named after his uncle.

JEAN FAURE, BROTHER OF PIERRE FAURE, SNR.

We have ample evidence to show that Jean (John) Faure was also a brother of Pierre Faure, Snr. In the Vestry Book of King William Parish, Jean and Pierre Faure are on the list of Tithables for the year 1713, and in 1717 Daniel Faure is included.

There is no grant of land recorded in the Land Office to John Faure until the year 1742, when in conjunction with Thomas Vann he was granted 178 acres in Henrico county. (Book 20, page 339.) In the County Records for Goochland, we derive the information that Pierre and Jean were brother, viz.:

"Conveyance from Peter Ford, Snr., King William Parish, Goochland county, planter, 7 March, 1728, to my dear and well beloved brother John Ford of the Parish of St. James, county afsd., 150 acres of land in sd. Parish of St. James."

(Recorded 18 March, 1728. Book I, page 66.)

This gift of land did not remain long in the possession of John Faure, as witness the following.

"Conveyance dated 12 May, 1729, from John Fourd, Parish of St. James, Goochland, planter, to Joseph Bingle, Parish of King William, same county, for twenty pounds, 150 acres of land in said county, beginning at the upper survey made by Peter Fourd and given to John Fourd."

(Book I, page 78.)

From the Parish Register of Manniken Town we find the following entries:

1 March, 1721-2. Jean Faure, godfather to Elizabeth Morriset. (Page 17.)

12 Dec., 1728, was born a boy to Jean Faure. (Page 82.)

There are no further entries in the Parish Register under the name of John Faure. It is evident that after selling the land, the gift of his brother, that John moved into Henrico county, where he died about the year 1748.

WILL OF JOHN FORE.

In the name of God, Amen.

I, John Fore, of King William Parish, county of Henrico, being very sick, do make this my last will and testament, etc.:

I give to my loving wife Mary the use of the plantation I now live on during her widowhood, and the use of all my slaves and personal estate until my children come of lawful age.

ITEM. I give to my daughter Elizabeth forty pounds, to be raised out of my estate, and a bed and a cow and a calf.

ITEM. I give to my daughter Mary a negro girl named Sarah, and a bed and a cow and calf.

ITEM. I give to my son John all my lands that I am possessed of and the land I agreed with Captain John Nash for, I give to him and his heirs.

I appoint my wife Mary my whole extx. and Robert Goode, my truly friend, to be guardian to my children.

In witness this 16 day of November, 1747.

JOHN [X] FORE.
His Mark.

Witnesses:
    William Scott,
    John Morriset,
    Walter Scott.

Probated by Mary Fore, the widow, the 1st Monday in July, 1748.

Henrico C. C. Book 1748-50, pages 5 and 6.

It will be seen that from existing records, John Faure, the brother of Peter, married a Mary ———, by whom he had issue:

    I. John, probably born 12 Dec., 1728.
    II. Elizabeth.
    III. Mary.

There is nothing further concerning the children of John Faure in the records of Henrico county, and it is likely they removed with other members of the family to Buckingham county.

(Continued)

ORANGE COUNTY MARRIAGE BONDS.

July 22, 1784. Samuel Grant and Lidia Craig. Security, Elijah Craig.

Jan. 8, 1784. Thomas Gillock and Elizabeth Morgan. Security, Joseph Thomas.

Oct. 18, 1785. Nathaniel Gordon and Mary Gordon. Security, David Hessing.

Mar. 15, 1785, William Goodall and Lucy Davis, daughter of Jonathan Davis. Security, John Davis.

Mar. 11, 1785. John Franklyne and Mary Pearson. Security, William Milligan.

Dec. 12, 1785. William Foard and Ann Moore. Security, Reuben Boston.

Dec. 12, 1784. Reuben Finnel and Elizabeth Bowen, daughter of Henry Bowen. Security, Catlet James.

Jan. 17, 1785. Richard Embre and Judith Payne. Security, George Payne.

April 28, 1785. John Eastin and Sarah Griffith. Security, David Griffith.

Sept. 7, 1785. Lavey Derey and Ann Wye. Security, James Head.

Aug. 28, 1785. James Davis and Ann Modiset, daughter of Mary Modiset. Security, Patrick Cochran.

Jan. 31, 1785. William Daniel and Mary Gaines. Security, Henry Chiles.

Aug. 1, 1785. Daniel Cowgill and Betsey Martin, consent of mother Ann Bowen. Security, John Bowen.

June 13, 1785. William Cook and Susannah Garton, daughter of Uriah Garton. Security, William Page.

Feb. 7, 1785. John Conner and Mary Lancaster, daughter of Robert Lancaster, who gives security.

Jan. 29, 1785. Ralph Cogwell and Sarah Reynolds.

Jan. 27, 1785. John Beckham and Mary Smith. Security, Henry Smith.

Sept. 1, 1785. Benj. Bragg and Polly Twentyman. Security, William Jamison.

Dec. 22, 1785. Sam'l. Brooking and Mary Taylor. Security, Chapman Taylor.

Nov. 23, 1784. William Brockman and Mary Smith. Security, George Smith.

Sept. 22, 1785. John Sams and Mary Bledsoe. Security, Aaron Bledsoe.

Aug. 19, 1784. David Thompson and Elizabeth Brockman. Security, Saul Brockman.

Aug. 13, 1784. Aaron Reynolds and Caty Chambers. Security, James Adams.

Feb. 28, 1785. James Wright and Sarah Rouser. Security, Luke Jennings.

Nov. 8, 1785. John Pendleton and Elizabeth Taylor. Security, James Taylor.

Aug. 22, 1785. Charles Neale and Ann Miller, daughter of Robert Miller. Security, Francis Collins.

Nov. 7, 1785. Henry Long and Lucy Mansfield. Security, John Long.

Mar. 9, 1785. Caleb Lindsey and Sally Stevens, daughter of John Stevens.

Dec. 21, 1784. Robert Leake and Susannah Leake. Security, Lewis Willis.

June 17, 1785. Kendall Lee and Sarah Gordon. Security, James Gordon.

Dec. 15, 1785. Sabert King and Mary Wayt, daughter of James Wayt.

Sept. 7, 1785. John Jones and Margaret Abell. Security, James Jones.

Sept. 7, 1785. James Jones and Caty Robinson, daughter of John Robinson. Security, John Jones.

Sept. 22, 1785. Edmond Henshaw and Mary Newman, daughter of James Newman, Snr. Security, James Newman, Jnr.

Oct. 28, 1785. Lewis Hensley and Mary Foster. Security, Esatham Snell.

Oct. 25, 1784. John Lamb and Nelly Lamb, daughter of John Lamb. Security, Thomas Lamb.

May 27, 1784. Jonathan Hiatt and Mary Conner, daughter of Rachel Conner. Security, Lewis Conner.

April 2, 1784. James Herring and Rachel Cofer, daughter of Judah and James Cofer. Security, Peter Rucker.

May 31, 1784. William Helm and Matilda Taliaferro, daughter of Francis Taliaferro. Security, Hay Taliaferro.

Aug. 21, 1784. Benj. Head, Jnr., and Margaret Gaar, daughter of Lewis Gaar. Security, William Head.

May 1, 1784. James Haney and Nancy Peters, daughter of Mathew Peters. Security, John Goodall.

"IMMIGRANTS TO VIRGINIA."

28 May, 1635

(Contd. from Vol. VI.)

Theis underwritten names are to be transported to Virginea, imbarqued in the SPEEDWELL, of London, Jo. Chappell, Master, being examined by the Minister of Gravesend of their conformitie to the orders and discipline of the Church of England, and have taken the oathe of allegeance.

Name	Years	Name	Years
Henry Beere	24	Ann Wyncott	16
Richard Morris	19	Elizabeth Pew	20
Wm. Shipman	22	Chri. Reinolds	24
William Pasford	19	Elizabeth Tuttell	25
Jo. Gilgate	22	John West	30
Richard Rowland	20	Nico. Tetloe	31
Jo. Curden	22	Nathl. Fairbrother	21
Jo. Harris	20	Jo. Watson	22
Edmond Clark	16	Robert Spynk	20
William Hynton	25	Thomas Childs	30
Richard Baylie	22	Tho. Romney	19
James Lowder	20	Christopher Peddington	18
Jeremy Burr	20	Jonas Smith	22
William Appleby	32	Jo. Mowson	22
Wm. Cunningham	21	William Spencer	17
William Stranghan	22	Christopher Metcalf	19
Richard Phillips	20	Richard Browne	19
Meleshus McKay	22	Robert Parker	21
Samuel Tyres	21	Thomas Willis	19
Thomas Busby	19	George Sympson	19
Thomas Robins	17	Arthur Saidwell	25
Jo. Turner	19	Richard Thomas	20
Jo. Bever	24	William Steevens	22
Edward Austin	26	Richard Harvy	32
Katherine Richards	19	Jo. Beeby	17
Elizabeth Biggs	10	Samuel Holmes	20

Jo. Talbott 27   Phillip Biggs ....6 mo.

Thomas Greene 24   Frances Langworth 25

Marie Sedgwick 20   Abram Poore 20

Dorothy Wyncott 40

(Continued.)

Virginia County Records

Published Quarterly

CONTENTS

Virginia County Records

QUARTERLY MAGAZINE

VOL. VII   DECEMBER 1910   No. 4

INDEX TO LAND GRANTS

CHARLOTTE COUNTY

Book 36.

Book 37.

Book 38.

500	James Speed	1769	654
565	Robert Breedlove	1769	400
613	James Williams	1769	2280
699	Benedict Alderson	1769	1200
709	Wood Jones	1769	140
857	Drury Stith	1769	4200

Book 39.

103	James Jennings	1770	181
107	Thomas Norriss	1770	230
158	James Jennings	1770	333
197	James Jennings	1770	94
306	Clement & Thomas Reade	1771	410
326	John Sullivant	1771	435
397	James Martin	1771	137

Book 40.

506	Anthony Griffin	1771	1350
720	Charles Turnbull	1772	104
737	Thomas East	1772	250
738	Paul Carrington	1772	324
832	Thomas Boulden	1772	230
833	Alex. Trent	1772	450
880	Peter Chastain	1772	69
512	Charles Harway	1771	275

Book No. 41.

31	Edward Robertson	1772	160
53	Jeremiah White	1772	527
360	Thomas Jones	1773	384
363	Robert Jennings	1773	426

Book No. 42.

| 663 | Wm. Armistead | 1774 | 111 |

Book A.

48	Thomas Read	1779	63
120	Wm. Johnson	1779	326

Book B.

21	Thomas Read	1779	31700
314	Francis Foster	1780	400
332	Thomas Read	1780	50

Book C.

373	John Bruce	1781	400

Book D.

6	James Speed	1780	397
341	William Bouton	1780	342
596	Thomas Rodgers	1781	380

Book E.

74	James Speed	1780	397
507	Lewis Deupree	1780	400
727	Thomas Boulden, Jr	1780	436
898	William Walton	1780	400

Book G.

141	Mack Goode	1782	409

Book I.

177	John Johns	1783	97

Book N.

16	Francis Walthall	1784	400

Book O.

343	John Beasley	1785	145½

Book V.

753	John Norris, Jr	1785	422

Book 18.

494 Wm. Carleton 1788   448

Book 21.

137 Wm. Davenport 1789   230

Book 22.

163 John Hay 1790   300
405 John H. Overstreet, heir to Wm. Overstreet,
        decd. 1790   1064
534 Nath'l Manson 1790   550

Book 24.

68 John Blankenship 1791   92

Book 25.

608 Charles Harris 1792   58

Book 27.

304 Thos. Parsons 1792   500

Book 28.

232 Levi Blankenship 1793   385
446 Levi Blankenship 1793   95
661 John Sandefer 1793   250
681 John Sandefer 1793   158

Book 29.

236 Wm. Dabbs, Jr......................1793   3624
252 Levi Blankenship 1793   72

Book 30.

296 Thos. Read 1794   740
503 Francis Barret 1794   367

Book 31.

187 John Harvie 1794   826
287 Richard Stone 1794   91
635 Benj. Marshall 1794   20

Book 32.

Book 33.

Book 34.

Book 35.

Book 36.

Book 37.

Book 38.

Book 39.

GLOUCESTER COUNTY.

Book 2.

Book 3.

166	Thos. Leechman and John Bennett.....1652	200
166	Capt. Francis Morgan and Ralph Green..1652	500
191	Col. Wm. Taylor 1653	1050
128	Isaac Richeson 1652	300
193	Rich'd Barnhouse, Jr................1653	200
194	Capt. Francis Morgan 1652	510
197	Peter Knight 1652	700
203	Wm. Ginsey 1652	302
204	Mrs. Anna Barnett 1652	1000
211	Anthony Langestone 1653	1303
213	Henry Soanes 1653	700
223	Wm. Coale 1653	100
223	John Hansford 1653	950
227	John Lewistone 1653	400
233	Wm. Wyatt 1653	400
237	Maj. Wm. Lewis 1654	640
237	Same 1654	1200
238	Same 1654	200
239	Anne Barnett ... .——	900
289	Rich'd Wilchin 1654	300
304	Col. Humphry Higginson and Thos. Higginson, son of sd. Col. Higginson......1654	800
318	Christopher Regault 1654	600
320	Edw. Simpson 1654	600
322	Humphrey Dennis 1654	200
326	Thos. Breeman 1654	600
326	Abraham Moon 1654	300
337	John Woodward 1655	500
337	Col. Rich'd Lee 1655	200
337	Capt. Robert Abrall.................1654	600
338	Geo. Moseley 1655	100
338	Thos. Peck 1655	1000
340	Peter Ford 1655	500
341	Sam'l Sollace and Robt. Trolwer.......1655	900
342	Sam'l Sollace 1655	352
350	Thos. Ballard 1655	1000
362	Hy. Huberd 1655	350
369	Thos. Hancks 1653	100

| 369 | Ralph Green ....1653 | 400 |
| 375 | Robert Huber ....1654 | 300 |

Book 4.

9	John Lewis, Jr........................1655	250
33	Rich'd Barnhouse, Jr................1655	200
38	Hy. Huberd 1655	250
47	Col. Rich'd Lee 1656	5
47	Wm. and Hancock Lee, sons of Col. Rich'd Lee 1656	850
76	Major Wm. Lewis 1656	1200
79	Ralph Green 1656	400
82	Thos. Bell 1656	134
106	Thos. Breamor 1656	300
122	Oliver Green 1657	450
150	Col. John West 1657	1000
157	Wm. Newman 1657	400
184	Capt. John Smith 1657	500
211	Thos. Graves 1657	55
212	Same 1657	240
229	Christopher Abbott 1657	350
236	Col. Hugh Gwin 1657	165
241	Geo. Poindexter and Geo. Thompson....1657	350
253	Lawrence Smith 1657	119
252	Capt. Augustine Warner 1657	348
266	Gilbert Medcalf 1657	500
304	John Champman 1657	250
312	Ralph Green 1658	1100
314	Hy. Forrest 1658	700
330	Michael Grafton 1658	200
377	Rich'd Dudley 1659	639
379	Cuthbert Potter 1659	5380
391	Edmund Peters 1659	442
407	John Green 1661	350
419	Edw. Wyatt 1662	1230
439	Robert Gregg and Edw. Wyatt........1662	370
464	Mrs. Avarila Curtis..................1661	410
523	Isaac Richardson 1661	300

523	Thomas Graves	1661	55
525	John Chapman	1661	250
525	Henry Huberd	1661	250
530	Thos. Graves	1661	240
530	Hugh Gwynn	1661	2000
533	Wm. Roberts	1661	200
534	Mrs. Ann Barnard	1661	900
534	Sam'l Sollis and Robt. Tolliver	1661	900
536	Sam'l Sollis, son of Sam'l Sollis, decd	1661	352
573	Eliz. Lawson	1662	1400
577	Ralph Greene	1662	1100
577	Same	1662	500

Book 5.

47	Edward Roe	1664	375
59	Wm. Corderoy	1664	400
84	Thos. Royston	1662	270
112	Rich'd Young	1665	1700
123	Jas. Bradbury	1662	250
152	—— Camfield	1663	400
168	Henry Carbell	1662	600
172	Wm. Hayward	1662	400
175	Wm. Corderoy	1662	120
177	John Fleet	1662	300
177	Rich'd Anderson	1662	200
194	Francis Ironmonger	1665	666
250	Geo. Billips	1663	250
252	Edw. Teale	1663	180
280	John Read	1662	145
286	Wm. Wyatt	1663	400
291	John Davis	1664	750
296	Robert Bryan	——	276
298	Edmund Peters	1662	442
333	Robert Lee	1662	542
335	Thomas Rines	1663	300
350	Ralph Harwood and Benj. Birch	1663	600
369	Robt. Coleman	1662	110

371	Ralph Ambery	1662	183
377	John Pate	1662	200
407	Wm. Ironmonger	1664	350
411	Lewis Day	1664	400
428	Charles Roane	1664	200
435	Thos. Dale	1664	350
437	Joseph Smith	1664	134
455	Gilbert Medcalfe	1664	810
473	Thos. Todd	1665	700
479	Rich'd Dudley	1665	455
503	Rich'd Renshaw	1664	300
508	Thos. Morris	1665	50
523	Robt. Bristow	1665	398
568	Wm. Claw	1665	200
573	Major John Smith	1665	500
573	Wm. Thornton	1665	164
574	Mr. Thos. Vicars, clerk	1665	650
586	John Read	1666	300
586	Abraham Jorsson, Jr	1665	985
594	John Pate	1662	200
594	John Pate	1666	300
595	John Okeham	1666	200
597	Chas. Roane	1665	100
598	Justinian Aylmer	1666	495
607	Robert Bristow	1666	184
615	Wm. Todd	1666	500
616	Major Thos. Walker	1665	2350
648	Guy Knight	1666	400
654	Col. Francis Willis	1666	100
667	Thos. Boswell	1666	100

Book 6.

23	John Benson	1666	140
25	Edw. Trate	1666	276
26	Oliver Green	1666	770
34	Robt. Coleman	1672	200
41	Lawrence Smith	1666	807
41	John Wray	1666	240

42	David Munorgon 1666	696
53	Rich'd Farthingale, Rich'd Barringham and	
	James Forsith 1671	800
60	Alex. Murray 1672	704
72	John Benson 1667	366
72	Thos. Wisdom 1667	127
74	John Walter 1667	423
74	Thos. Jonas 1667	74
75	John Kerby 1671	130
83	Michaell Crafton 1667	720
91	Thos. Colles 1667	200
97	Geo. Curtis 1667	1100
98	Thos. Colles 1667	137
100	Anne Boram 1667	148
100	Roger Leonard 1667	300
102	Wm. Roberts 1667	170
102	Hy. Prouse 1667	200
102	Dunken Bohona and John Mechen 1667	220
103	Jas. Ransome 1667	300
103	Hy. Singleton 1667	300
103	Rich'd Dudley 1667	300
104	John Sanderson 1667	300
104	Rich'd Dudley 1667	300
130	Francis Campfield 1668	314

KING GEORGE COUNTY RECORDS

Will of Henry Turner, Hanover Parish, King George Co., ———, 1751. My wife Elizabeth; my son Thomas to be left in the care of my honoured father Thomas Turner. If my son Thomas should die without issue all the land in King George County left to my brother Thomas Turner's son Charles of Spottsylvania County, and all land in Prince William County to my nephews Harry Dixon and Turner Dixon.

Will of John Tyler of King George County, dated 4 November, 1755, probated 2 June, 1757.　My wife Mary; my grandson Tyler Waugh; my son-in-law, William Waugh; grandsons William and Thomas Waugh; my granddaughters Priscilla and Mellion Waugh; my daughter Margaret.

Will of Thomas Turner, King George County; no date; probated 4 May, 1758.　My son-in-law Captain Edward Dixon and his sons Harry and Turner Dixon; grandson Thomas Turner; grandson Henry Turner; granddaughter Sally Turner; my niece Ann wife of John Wren and her children; whereas my son Harry by his last will directed that his son Thomas should have the best education, I therefore direct that all my grandsons shall have the same; my niece Ann's son John; my daughter Mary Turner.　Codicil dated 18 February, 1757.　To grandson Harry Turner then under age land in Prince William and Westmoreland Counties.

Will of Aaron Grigsby, King George County, dated 5 Jan., 1764; probated 5 April, 1764.　All my estate to my wife Berlinda.

Will of George Morton, King George County, dated 8 July, 1765; probated 7 August, 1766.　My sons John and George; my son Robert Baylor Morton; daughter Frances Hedgman; wife Lucy Morton; son Joseph.

Will of Howson Hooe, King George County, dated 16 December, 1773; probated 4 January, 1781.　My wife Ann Frances; son William; son Bernard; son Howson; son John; son Harris.

Will of Esther Tyler, widow, King George County, 12 May, 1770.　Son William Tyler; son James Tyler; daughter Blanche Tyler; brother Mr. Joseph Jones to be executor.

Deed of conveyance dated 21 March, 1726, from Rice Rooe and Catherine his wife, of King George County, conveying a part of the land in same County, which was sold by John Reynolds to Mr. Richard Taliaferro, and

which from the said Richard Taliaferro descended to
his son Richard Taliaferro, Jnr., brother to the aforesaid Catherine Hooe, who inherited upon the death of
the said Richard Taliaferro, Jnr.

Sarah, wife of Thomas Turner alive in 1729.

Will of Seymour Hooe, King George County, dated 13
October, 1780; probated 3 April, 1783. My wife Sarah;
my son Alexander Seymour Hooe; my unborn child;
my daughter Lucy Thornton Hooe; my brother Gerrard
Hooe; my nephew John Storke.

Will of William Tyler, King George County, dated 11
August, 1783; probated 1 April, 1784. My wife Sarah;
Elizabeth Gray Dudley, daughter of Elizabeth Pittman
Dudley; my brother James Tyler.

Will of Gerrard Hooe, King George County; dated 29 December, 1785; probated 1 June, 1786. My wife Sarah;
the rest of my estate to be divided amongst my unmarried children; my son-in-law George Mason to be executor.

Thomas Turner, Esq., and Jane his wife alive in 1774.

At a Court held 19 May, 1721, the estate of Richard Taliaferro to be inventoried and his will probated upon
petition of Thomas Turner and Martha his wife.

At a Court held 26 September, 1723. Thomas Turner produced his commission as Clerk.

NORTHAMPTON COUNTY MARRIAGE BOND
(Continued from page 44)

Sept. 22, 1787. John Carpenter and Lucy Gault.
Nov. 29, 1788. Hillary Clegg and Peggy Knight, dau. of
William Knight, decd.
Dec. 20, 1788. John Caple and Ann, dau. of Paul Phaben,
decd.
Aug. 11, 1790. John Collins and Nancy Sobers.
Nov. 24, 1791. Mathew Costin and Mary Joyne, widow.
Jan. 13, 1791. Severn Chum and Tamar M———, who
was 21 years old the 2 Jan., 1791.

Jan. 12, 1791.	William Costin and Lucretia Dixon.
Apr. 10, 1792.	Samuel Cullen and Polly Rippen.
Aug. 6, 1793.	John Costin and Elizabeth Fletcher, dau. of Joshua Fletcher.
Sept. 27, 1793.	Caleb Core and Sarah Parramore.
Oct. 9. 1794.	Major Clegg and Patience Benthall.
Dec. 20, 1794.	Ralph Collins and Tamar Bingham.
Jan. 3, 1795.	Lighty Collins and Leah Drighouse.
Jan. 19, 1796.	Samuel Costin and Polly Roberts.
Sept. 12, 1796.	John Collins and Grace Costin.
Nov. 14, 1796.	John Carpenter and Ada Floyd, dau. of Mathew.
Nov. 2, 1796.	Thomas Clay and Sally Freshwater, dau. of William.
Dec. 20, 1796.	Richard Coleburn and Beggy Bool.
Mar. 13, 1797.	William Carmine and Nancy Belote.
Dec. 24, 1798.	Robert Clegg and Polly Bloxom.
June 28, 1798.	Elijah Carmine and Camilla White.
July 21, 1798.	Abraham Costin, Jnr., and Peggy Costin dau. of Francis.
Mar. 11, 1799.	John Carpenter, Jnr., and Fanny Scott, dau. of John.
Jan. 31, 1799.	Joseph Collins and Betty Anderson.
Dec. 9, 1799.	John Cook and Molly Traves.
May 22, 1800.	John Cotterell and Betsy Fletcher.
Jan. 18, 1800.	Major Clegg and Nancy M———.
Sept. 5, 1800.	John Costin and Nancy Evans.
May 25, 1801.	John Carmine and Polly Abdell.
Feb. 14, 1705-6.	Benjamin Dalby and Ann Stott, widow.
Oct. 1, 1709.	William Dunn and Mary Godfrey.
Nov. 30, 1722.	Reverend Thomas Dell and Mary Reeve.
Aug. 18, 1722.	Ricketts Dunton and Ann Jacob, widow.
Sept. 10, 1740.	Col. George Dashiell of Somerset Co., Md., and Elizabeth Fairfax.
Sept. 29, 1743.	James Delpreach and Peggy Samson, widow.

Mar. 11, 1744.   Levin Dunwood of Maryland and Isabel Stringer.

May 17, 1756.   Waterfield Dunton and Susanna Waterfield, dau. of Jacob.

Oct. 6, 1750.   Elias Dunton and Esther Waterfield, widow.

Aug. 14, 1759.   Isaac Dolby and Peggy Mathews, dau. of John Custis Mathews.

July 7, 1759.   William Drummond and Nancy Dunton, dau. of Elias.

May 19, 1764.   Jacob Dolby and Jane Luke, widow.

May 24, 1763.   Jacob Dunton and Betty Satchell, dau. of Southy.

Aug. 12, 1760.   George Dashiell and Rose Fisher, dau. of Maddox Fisher, decd.

Feb. 25, 1769.   John Dalby, Jnr., and Susanna Jacob, dau. of Isaac.

Jan. 14, 1772.   William Downing and Martha Jacob, dau. of Philip, decd.

May 5, 1770.   Benjamin Dixon and Elizabeth Nelson.

Oct. 10, 1769.   John Dalby and Keziah Westerhouse.

Aug. 19, 1772.   Thomas Dalby and Margaret Haze, dau. of John, decd.

Oct. 21, 1772.   Elisha Dowty and Elishe Jacob, dau. of Thomas.

Nov. 7, 1772.   Henry Dalby and Rachel Andrews.

Sept. 7, 1774.   Rickards Dunton, Jnr., and Sophia Harmanson.

Apr. 20, 1774.   Peter Dickerson and Mary Waterfield, widow.

Dec. 31, 1777.   John Darby (Dalby?) and Esther Harmanson, dau. of John Harmanson, Snr.

Sept. 15, 1778.   Benjamin Dunton and Ann Jacob, dau. of Hancock.

Dec. 31, 1778.   Levin Davis and Susanna Westerhouse.

July 15, 1778.   Addison Dowty and Tabitha Milby.

July 13, 1779.	Addison Dowty and Seymour Heath, dau. of William.
May 26, 1779.	Michael Dunton and Rosey Mathews, dau. of John Custis Mathews, decd., and Martha Mathews.
Jan. 22, 1780.	Michael Dunton and Ann Notingham, widow.
April 4, 1780.	Spencer Dalby and Nancy Watson, dau. of Littleton.
Jan. 1, 1780.	John Dalby and Leah Dunton.
Sept. 11, 1781.	John Dixon and Bridget Thomas, dau. of John.
May 14, 1782.	John Darby and Esther Christian.
Sept. 22, 1783.	Christopher Dixon and Sabra Simpkins.
Feb. 7, 1783.	Thomas Downs and Anne Williams.
Dec. 29, 1784.	William Dixon and Esther Kendall.
June 25, 1785.	Severn Dunton and Agnes Grice.
Feb. 12, 1785.	William Dolby and Sarah Eshon.
April 4, 1785.	Isaac Dunton and Elizabeth Toleman.
Dec. 15, 1786.	John Dennis and Susanna Widgen.
Aug. 2, 1786.	John Dixon and Lucretia Costin.
Aug. 4, 1786.	Robert Davis and Sarah Andrews.
July 19, 1786.	Benjamin Dolby and Mary Core.
Mar. 8, 1787.	Peter Dowty and Sinah Edmunds.
Mar. 14, 1787.	William Dixon and Betty Dunton, widow of Jacob.
May 9, 1787.	Henry Dalby and Susannah Sturgis.
Jan. 12, 1788.	Michael Dennis and Milly Jackson.
Dec. 3, 1788.	Littleton Dennis of Worcester Co., Md., and Elizabeth Upshur, dau. of John Upshur, Snr.
Apr. 24. 1788.	Joseph Dennis and Lavinia Berch.
Aug. 29, 1788.	William Dalby and Martha Bool, widow of Nicholas.
Sept. 24, 1788.	Archibald Dowty and Nancy Edmunds, dau. of David, decd.
Nov. 16, 1789.	James Dalby and Ann Griffith.

Oct.   8, 1789.   Thomas Dalby and Catherine Harmanson, dau. of John, decd.
Dec. 17, 1789.   Benjamin Dalby and Sarah Bull.
May   2, 1789.   Joseph Dalby and Bridget Mulhollums.
Nov. 10, 1789.   Jacob Dalby and Abigail Bell.
Aug. 17, 1790.   Thomas Dixon and Elizabeth Holms, widow.
Mar. 20, 1790.   John Dalby, Jnr., and Elizabeth Barlow, widow of Thomas.
Dec. 20, 1790.   Southey Dunton and Peggy Dalby, dau. of John.
Dec. 21, 1790.   Michael Douty and Peggy Jones.

VIRGINIA REVOLUTIONARY PENSIONERS

(Continued from page 52.)

Lucy Southworth, Caroline County, aged 75 years.
George Saunders, Caroline County, aged 79 years.
Bartholomew Taylor, Caroline County, aged 78 years.
Catlett Thomas, Caroline County, aged 77 years.
James Thomas, Caroline County, aged 75 years.
William Tucker, Caroline County, aged 75 years.
Agnes Yarborough, Caroline County, aged 74 years.
Elizabeth Ashworth, Charlotte County, aged 69 years.
Joanna Bouldin, Charlotte County, aged 88 years.
Martha Brown, Charlotte County, aged 78 years.
Clement Carrington, Charlotte County, aged 77 years.
Susan Davis, Charlotte County, aged 91 years.
Solomon H. Elam, Charlotte County, aged 82 years.
David Bartee, Charlotte County, aged 74 years, residing with George Harvey.
William P. Hamlett, Charlotte County, aged 81 years.
Daniel Hendrick, Charlotte County, aged 78 years.
Ambrose Hailey, Charlotte County, aged 82 years.
James Mullins, Charlotte County, aged 89 years, residing with James Johnson.

James Rudder. Charlotte County, aged 80 years, residing with Major J. Drury.

Nancy Mathews, Charlotte County, aged 80 years.

Isaac Robertson, Snr., Charlotte County, aged 86 years.

Isaac Smith, Charlotte County, aged 74 years.

Agnes St. John, Charlotte Co., aged 75 years, residing with Jacob A. St. John.

Lucy Spencer, Charlotte County, aged 80 years, residing with William W. Spencer.

Joseph Sammons, Charlotte County, aged 55 years.

William Skelton, Charlotte County, aged 83 years.

Elizabeth Tombs, Charlotte County, aged 75 years, residing with Charles Tombs.

William Walker, Charlotte County, aged 78 years.

William Hill, Chesterfield County, aged 80 to 90 years.

Jordan Anderson, Chesterfield Co., aged 80 to 90 years.

Nathaniel Puckett, Chesterfield County, aged 85 years.

Moses Ferguson, Chesterfield County, aged 79 years.

William Goode, Snr., Chesterfield County, aged 79 years.

John Bass, Snr., Chesterfield County, aged 79 years.

John Spears, Chesterfield County, aged 80 years.

Jacob Flournoy, Chesterfield County, aged 79 years.

John Dyson, Chesterfield County, aged 78 years.

Isham Andrews, Chesterfield County, aged 93 years.

Ezekiel Perkinson, Chesterfield County, aged 82 years.

Levi Newby, Chesterfield County, aged 85 years.

Thomas Newby, Chesterfield County, aged 79 years.

Thomas Gregory, Snr., Chesterfield County, aged 88 years.

Catharine Allen, Culpepper County, aged 79 years.

Nancy Bailey, Culpepper County, aged 75 years, residing with Armistead Bailey.

John Creel, Culpepper County, (age not given).

Sarah Calvin, Culpepper County, aged 78 years.

John Cannaday, Culpepper County, aged 77 years.

Lucy Pettit, Culpepper County, aged 78 years, residing with John L. Conner.

Elizabeth Edwards, Culpepper County, aged 90 years.

John Freeman, Culpepper County, aged 83 years.
Zachariah Griffin, Culpepper County, aged 79 years.
Gabriel Gray, Culpepper County, aged 77 years.
Humphrey Hill, Culpepper County, aged 77 years.
Julius Hunt, Culpepper County, aged 78 years.
John Hall, Culpepper County, aged 79 years.
William Jett, Culpepper County, aged 77 years.
William Lewis, Culpepper County, aged 77 years.
Mary Lambkin, Culpepper County, aged 78 years.
Hannah Clark, Culpepper County, aged 87 years, residing
   with Madden Willis.
Abner Newman, Culpepper County, aged 85 years.
Richard Payne, Snr., Culpepper County, aged 77 years.
Reuben Rosson, Culpepper County, aged 87 years.
Randolph Stallard, Culpepper County, aged 83 years, resid-
   ing with Randolph Stallard, Jnr.
Philip Slaughter, Culpepper County, aged 82 years, residing
   with Philip C. Slaughter.
Peter Triplett, Culpepper County, aged 88 years.
Almond Vaughan, Culpepper County, aged 84 years.
Isiah Welsh, Culpepper County (age not given).
Bartlett Cox, Cumberland County, aged 85 years.
Richard Taylor, Cumberland County, aged 84 years.
Daniel Tolty, Cumberland County, aged 75 years.
James Morton, Cumberland County, aged 83 years, resid-
   ing with Wm. S. Morton.
William Walker, Cumberland County, aged 83 years.
James Bishop, Snr., Dinwiddie County, aged 79 years.
Samuel Major, Dinwiddie County, aged 78 years.
George Simmons, Dinwiddie County, aged 83 years.
Thomas Wilkinson, Dinwiddie County, aged 82 years.
Josiah Grigg, Dinwiddie County, aged 79 years, residing
   with Theodorick H. Grigg.
Joel Sturdivant, Snr., Dinwiddie County, aged 78 years.
Claiborne Elder, Dinwiddie County, aged 82 years.
Bolling Wells, Dinwiddie County, aged 81 years.
Peter Epes, Dinwiddie County, aged 81 years.
William Nunally, Dinwiddie County, aged 84 years.

James Boss, Dinwiddie County, aged 80 years, residing with
    Jane Boss.
James Spiceley, Dinwiddie County, aged 78 years.
Joseph Scott, Dinwiddie County, aged 55 years.
William R. Cheeves, Dinwiddie County, aged 55 years.
John Armstrong, Essex County, aged 78 years, residing with
    Joseph Armstrong.
Carter Croxton, Essex County, aged 80 years.
Benjamin H. Munday, Essex County, aged 77 years.
Reuben Atkinson, Essex County, aged 90 years, residing
    with Robert Atkinson.
Thomas Cognell, Essex County, aged 78 years.
Ann D. Butler, Essex County, aged 80 years, residing with
    Lewis Warner.
Daniel Saunders, Fairfax County, aged 90 years.
Ann Blackweel, Fauquier County, aged 79 years, residing
    with James Balckweel.
Susan Burke, Fauquier County, aged 96 years.
Robert Combs, Fauquier County, aged 87 years.
Anthony Ethel, Fauquier County, aged 83 years.
George Purcell, Fauquier County, aged 90 years, residing
    with William German.
George Green, Fauquier County, aged 80 years, residing
    with George J. Green.
Martha Howell, Fauquier County, aged 70 years.
Alexander Jeffries, Fauquier County, aged 77 years, resid-
    ing with George Jeffries.
Hannah Lear, Fauquier County, aged 70 years, residing
    with James Lear.
Elizabeth Maffett, Fauquier County, aged 82 years, resid-
    ing with John A. Maffett.
William Pattie, Fauquier County, aged 78 years.
Martha Roach, Fauquier County, aged 80 years, residing
    with James M. Roach.
William Rawles, Fauquier County, aged 80 years.
Michael Wiser, Fauquier County, aged 75 years.
Rose Merry, Fauquier Co., aged 75 years, residing with
    Samuel Wharton.

John Welch, Fauquier County, aged 68 years, residing with William A. Bowen.

Amie Claggett, Fauquier County, aged 68 years, residing with Ferd. Claggett.

Elizabeth Arrowsmith, Fauquier County, aged 75 years, residing with Day Mildred.

Ann Vowles, Fauquier County, aged 88 years, residing with Newton Vowles.

Frances Walker, Fauquier County, aged 80 years, residing with Solomon Walker.

Stephen Mayo, Fluvanna County, aged 82 years.

Isaac Lucado, Fluvanna County, aged 82 years, residing with Littleberry Lucado.

Hopper Ward, Fluvanna County, aged 88 years, residing with Archibald Creary.

Martin Faris, Fluvanna County, aged 77 years.

Charles Clements, Snr., Fluvanna County, aged 81 years.

John S. Haislip, Fluvanna County, aged 80 years.

Daniel Thacker, Fluvanna County, aged 81 years.

Zaccheus Granger, Fluvanna County, aged 79 years, residing with Allen T. Watson.

Jesse Saunders, Fluvanna County, aged 88 years.

Richard Cawthorn, Snr., Fluvanna County, aged 76 years.

Thomas Shores, Fluvanna County, aged 85 years.

Jesse Wood, Fluvanna County, aged 86 years.

John Maddox, Fluvanna County, aged 76 years.

Nathaniel Harlow, Fluvanna County, aged 97 years.

(Continued.)

IMMIGRANTS TO VIRGINIA.

6 June, 1635.

Theis under written names are to be transported to Virginea, imbarqued in the "Thomas & John," Richard Lambard, Master, being examined by the Minister of Gravesend concerning their conformitie to the orders and discipline of the Church of England, and tooke the oath of allegeance.

Years.   Years.

Richard Pew	23	Jo. Dickenson	22
Richard Maynwrite	24	Thomas Bell	17
Chri. Houghton	19	William Bett	20
Richard Jones	24	James Cross	27
Francis Garrett	25	Silas Foster	22
Richard Dally	18	Edward Mountford	20
Thomas Terry	25	Henry Newby	24
Charles Wyngate	22	John Eden	19
John Hampton	30	Thomas Sherley	23
John Evans	22	John Thomson	24
John Singleton	18	Henry Warren	15
George Dickenson	19	John Wilkinson	28
George Hawkins	18	Ralph Hudson	17
Henry Rastell	30	Thomas Allin	33
Francis Spight	21	William Jones	17
William Aymie	26	Thomas Sharples	23
William Hynton	20	William White	22
John Edwardson	22	James Sherborne	15
Thomas Mann	23	William Gardener	15
Robert Aldred	24	John Robinson	19
Zachary Taylor	24	Robert Turner	16
Humphrey Grudge	21	John Moss	21
William White	22	Jane Wilkinson	20
Joseph Monuvs	21	Ann Brookes	18
Christopher Wheatley	28	Katherine Wiseman	19
Robert Heed	27	Jane Scott	19
Edward Coles	20	Jane Catesby	20
Morris Jones	28	James Powell	12
Wardin Fositt	22	William Mann	25
Thos. Chamberlin	20	Thomas Warner	26
William Bead	15	Thomas Ram	19
Lawrence Platt	15	Griffin Jones	21
Robert Spencer	21	Thomas Tollie	17
Samuel Walden	16	William Jones	21
Henry Morley	25	Marmaduke Young	24
Ben Easy	13	George Kenyon	25

	Years		Years
Robert Sewar	23	William Clark	18
Owen Hughes	27	Thomas Clark	16
John Sutton	24	Giles Terry	33
Wm. Stonhouse	43	Edward Cressitt	20
Morris Parry	30	Thomas Waggitt	17
James Banks	30	Mary Ford	22
Edward Dix	19	Katherine Waterman	20
William Chaplin	18	Lawrence Preston	21
Jo. Shorter	26	William Wheatlie	17
Anth. Terry	50	William Lacy	18
Robert Willins	44	George Cobcraste	22
Thomas Rosdell	23	John Kenyon	21

(Continued)

ENGLISH DESCENT OF TAZEWELL FAMILY

The Tazewell family of Virginia descend from William Taswell of the County of Somerset. Four generations are to be found in the Visitation of London in 1664. (D. 19 fo. 88 b. Heralds Coll., London.)

The pedigree in the Visitation begins with James Tazewell of the County of Somerset. This Christian name is erroneously entered as "James" instead of "William," as the following entry of baptism in the parish register of Buckland Newton shows: "Julii, 1588. Vicesimo quinto die mensis praedicti baptizatus fuit Jacobus Taswell (sic) filius Will'mi Taswell de Buckland."

In the Heralds Visitations errors in Christian names are very frequent. The pedigree therefore begins with:

1. William Tazewell of the County of Somerset.
2. James Tazewell of Buckland in the County of Dorset, born July, 1588. His first wife Mary, daughter of ——— Hunt of Forston, Charminter, County of Dorset, died in 1659, and was buried at Haselbury Bryan, Dorset, in the registers of which parish is the following entry: "Burials, A. D. 1659, Maria uxor Jacobi Tazwell obiit 19 Jan." In the

"Autobiography of William Taswell, D.D. (his grandson),
published by the Camden Society in 1852, it is stated (p.
8) : "In the same year, 1662, my grandfather James Taswell of
Dorsetshire came to town, aged 74, born in the year 1588.
Staying a little time with us only, he soon returned into the
country, and took his own servant to wife; he begat a son
the same year of her. He departed this life 1663. On the
day he was celebrating his wife's birthday, he drank too
much wine, which threw him into a fever." By his will
(proved in the Archdeaconry Court of Dorset in 1663), in
which he is described as "James Taswell of Haselbury
Bryan," he gives "to my sonne James Taswell one shilling;
to my daughter Mary Young one shilling; to my kinsman
Ralphe Taswell one sute of aparell; to my kinsman Richard
Taswell one sute of aparell; all the rest of my goods move-
able and unmoveable I give and bequeath unto my wife
Aner whom I do make executrix of this my last will." It
appears by Hutchins History of Dorset that the Hunt family held the Manor of Forston. On the death in 1683 of
Anne, daughter and heiress of Henry Hunt, Esq., of Forston, the estate descended to her issue by her second husband, George Browne, Esq., a younger son of the Brownes
of Frampton.

3. James Tazewell of London, merchant, and of
Limington Manor, Somerset, married (1) 26 March, 1649,
Elizabeth, daughter of ——— Upsal of the County of Dorset (born 1624, died 1667), and (2) in 1673, Elizabeth,
daughter of John Kingsmill of Andover, Esq. (she died July,
1702, s.p.). James Tazewell died 26 March, 1683. In the
son's autobiography (William Tazewell, D.D.), we read:
"Not long after the barbarous murther of Charles the First
James Taswell married Elizabeth Upsal, a person accom-
plished as to her person, sensible, and of a very good extrac-
tion. He was a considerable merchant in the Isle of Wight,
and connected himself to her March 26, 1649. About the
end of March, 1655, James Taswell, Esq., retiring from the
Isle of Wight with his wife and three children, settled at a

seaport town, Brithamston, Sussex, where his mother-in-law, my grandmother, lived. In June, 1656, we took a journey to London. After residing in a house for the space of a year, in which time all of us were seized with the smallpox (1657), about the middle of summer we took a very grand house in Bear Lane, near the Custom House. In 1673 my father married Elizabeth Kingsmill of Andover, with a fortune of 600 pounds. In 1663 James Tazwell, who was seised of the Manor of South Brent, Somerset, and of was seised of the Manor of Douth Brent, Somerset, and of other lands in that county and in the adjoining county of Devon, purchased the Manor and advowson of Limington, Somerset. He rebuilt the Manor House at Limington in 1672. A stone with the name of "James Tazwell, arms and date 1672" which formerly appeared on the front of the old Manor House, is now in the possession of Mr. T. P. Taswell-Langmead. The children of James and Elizabeth Tazewell given in the Visitation are: James, son and heir aet, 14 years in 1664; William; Stephen; Thomas; Eliza; Mary; Hannah. Besides these children they had: "Maria, born 29 December, 1649, died aged 8 months; Elizabeth, born 7 July, 1653, died soon after; Ann, born November, 1659, died soon after; and Maria, born February, 1667, died soon after.

4. James Tazwell, eldest son and heir of James and Elizabeth, was born 20 February, 1650, and succeeded his father in the Manor of Limington. He married Ann, daughter of ―――― Kingsmil, by whom he had three sons and three daughters. The sons were:

(1) James, who d.s.p.

(2) John, who was M.A. of Christ Church, Oxford, was Vicar of Chewton, Somerset, and died without male issue.

(3) William Tazewell, baptized 17 July, 1690, immigrated to Virginia in 1715, where he married in 1721, Sophia, daughter of Henry Harmanson, by his wife Gertrude, daughter of Col. Southey Littleton. He died in 1752, leaving issue.

4. William Tazwell, D.D., second son of James and Elizabeth, was born 1 May, 1652, and was an eminent scholar and divine. Enrolled a King's Scholar of Westminster School, 1667; elected Student of Christ Church, Oxford, 1670; Professor of Greek, 1681; Rector of Woodnorton, Norfolk, 1691; Rector of St. Mary Newington, Surrey, 1698; Rector of St. Mary's, Birmingham, 1723. He died in 1731 and was buried in the Chancel of St. Mary's, Newington. He married 21 May, 1695, Frances, daughter and co-heir of Edward Lake, D.D., Archdeacon of Exeter, Chaplain and Tutor to the Princesses Mary and Anne, daughters of James II, and had issue.

4. Stephen Tazewell, the third son of James and Elizabeth, was born December, 1656; resided at Limington, and married Barbara, daughter of John Pinny of Hardington, Somerset (born 1673, died 18 June, 1706). He died in 1742, leaving issue, inter alios, a son William Taswell, born 6 March, 1705.

4. Thomas Tazewell, the fourth son of James and Elizabeth, was born 20 April, 1663, and died at the age of 9 months.

4. Elizabeth Tazwell, born 14 September, 1654; died in 1703, unmarried.

4. Mary Tazewell, born 6 May, 1658, died young.

4. Hannah Tazewell, born 30 January, 1660, married ——— Lockyer of Limington, and had issue.

EXTRACTS FROM THE REGISTER OF LIMINGTON, SOMERSET

John ye son of James and Mrs. Ann Tasewell was baptized Nov. 9, 1688.

Barbara ye daughter of Stephen Tazwell and Barbara his wife was baptized July 2, 1690.

William the son of James Tazwell and Ann his wife was baptized July 17, 1690.

June 30, 1692, was baptized Ann the daughter of James Tazewell, Gent., and Ann his wife, who was born on the 17 June, 1692.

August ye 18, 1693, was baptized Stephen ye son of Stephen and Barbara Tazewell.

January 29, 1694, was baptized Frances ye daughter of Mr. James Tazewell.

June ye 5, 1697, was baptized Elizabeth ye daughter of Mr. James and Mrs. Anne Tazewell.

June ye 9, 1697, was baptized Elizabeth, ye daughter of Mr. Stephen and Mrs. Barbara Tazewell.

Mary ye daughter of Mr. Stephen and Mrs. Barbara Tazewell was born the 29th and baptized on the 30th day of July, 1699.

Constance the daughter of James Tazewell, Esq., and Mrs. Ann Tazewell was born and baptized the 15th February, 1699-70.

John Pinney the son of Mr. Stephen and Mistress Barbara Tazewell was born the 26th day of March, 1701, and baptized 18 April, 1701.

James the son of Mr. Stephen and Mrs. Barbara Tazewell was born on the 26th of June, 1704, and baptized on the 10th July, 1704.

William the son of Stephen Tazwell was born on the 6th March, 1705.

Mrs. Elizabeth Tazewell was buryed on the 8th day of July, 1702.

Barbara the wife of Stephen Tazewell was buried on the 28th day of June, 1706.

The Tazewell arms as recorded at the College of Arms by George Harrison, Windsor Herald, in the year 1664:

Vaire purpure and ermine; on a chief gules a lion passant or.

Crest: A demi-lion purpure; in the paws a chaplet of eight roses gules.

VIRGINIA REVOLUTIONARY SOLDIERS

Watts, John, Captain, Contl. Line, 7 years' service.
Lee, Hy., Lieut.-Col., Contl. Line, 7 years' service.
Walker, Jeremiah, Private, Contl. Line, 3 years' service.
Green, Gabriel, Lieut., Contl. Line, 3 years' service.
Berry, Geo., Captain, Contl. Line, 3 years' service.
Gibson, John, Jr., Ensign, Contl. Line, 3 years' service.
Jones, Wm., Corporal, Contl. Line, 3 years' service.
Burnett, Jno., Private, Contl. Line, 3 years' service.
Rock, Jno., Private, Contl. Line, 3 years' service.
McCartney, Peter, Private, Contl. Line, 3 years' service.
Brown, Jonathan, Seaman, State Navy, 3 years' service.
Lewis Ambrose, Seaman, State Navy, 3 years' service.
Waters, Jas., Sergeant, Contl. Line, 3 years' service.
Belfield, Jno., Major, Contl. Line, 3 years' service.
Rose, Robt., Dr.-Surgeon, Contl. Line, 7 years' service.
Henderson, David, Midshipman, State Navy, 3 years' service.
Parker, Watts, Sergeant, Contl. Line, 3 years' service.
Grant, Danl., Gunner's Mate, 3 years' service.
Moore, Jno., Master, State Navy, 3 years' service.
Cox, Presly, Private, Contl. Line, 3 years' service.
Vaughan, Rich., Private, Contl. Line, 3 years' service.
Belcher, Robt., Private, Contl. Line, 3 years' service.
Biswell, Jno., Corporal, Contl. Line, 3 years' service.
Fear, Hamner, Private, State Line, 3 years' service.
Charles, Saml., Sergeant, Contl. Line, 3 years' service.
Barham, Moody, Private, State Line, 3 years' service.
Anderson, John, Sergeant, Contl. Line, 3 years' service.
Armond, Jno., Private, Contl. Line, 3 years' service.
Rose, Wm., Private, State Line, 3 years' service.
Rose, Jesse, Private, State Line, 3 years' service.
Kenton, Mark, Private, Contl. Line, 7 years' service.
Jordain, Jno., Private, Contl. Line, 3 years' service.
Culbertson, Jas., Captain, Contl. Line, 3 years' service.
Gray, Danl., Private, Contl. Line, 3 years' service.
Fuglar, Wm., Private, Contl. Line, 3 years' service.

Henshaw, Wm., Private, Contl. Line, 3 years' service.
Gains, John, Private, State Navy, 3 years' service.
Poplar, Hack, Seaman, State Navy, 3 years' service.
Pitman, Isaac, Sergeant, Contl. Line, 3 years' service.
Hopkins, Patk., Private, State Navy, 3 years' service.
Anglen, Isaac, Private, Contl. Line, 3 years' service.
Beal, Wm., Sergeant, Contl. Line, 3 years' service.
Poythress, Wm., Capt.-Lieut. Artillery, Contl. Line, 3 years'
    service.
Spencer, Abraham, Private, State Navy, for the war.
Flemings, Chas., Lieut.-Col., Contl. Line, 3 years' service.
Carter, Armestead, Private, Contl. Line, 3 years' service.
Carter, Robert, Sergeant, Contl. Line, 3 years' service.
Hannah, Robert, Private, Contl. Line, 3 years' service.
McGann, Jas., Private, Contl. Line, 3 years' service.
Haley, Wm., Private, Contl. Line, 7 years' service.
Ramsey, Francis, Private, Contl. Line, 3 years' service.
Magill, Chas., Major, State Line, 3 years' service.
Parker, Alex., Captain, Contl. Line, 8 years' service.
Bradley, Wm., Sergeant, Contl. Line, 3 years' service.
Kennedy, Wm., Private, Contl. Line, 3 years' service.
Jones, Saml., Corporal, Contl. Line, 3 years' service.
Sheldon, Thos. alias Chilton, Fifer-Major, Contl. Line, 8
    years' service.
Lee, Randolph, Private, State Line, 3 years' service.
Hughs, Joseph, Private, Contl. Line, 3 years' service.
Waters, Thos., Private, Contl. Line, 3 years' service.
Gold, Michael, Private, Contl. Line, 7 years' service.
Leonard, Robert, Private, Contl. Line, 7 years' service.
Slaven, Cornelius, Private, State Line, 3 years' service.
Gowin, Sherod, Private, Contl. Line, 3 years' service.
Dicky, Alex., Private, Contl. Line, 7 years' service.
Johnston, Thos., Private, Contl. Line, 3 years' service.
Morris, Jno., Private, Contl. Line, 3 years' service.
Hill, Hy., Private, State Line, 3 years' service.
Overton, Francis, Capt., Contl. Line, 3 years' service.
Cartwright, Jushman, Sergeant, Contl. Line, 7 years' service.
Finnell, Reuben, Private, Contl. Line, 3 years' service.

Parker, Josiah, Col., Contl. Line, 3 years' service.
Kelly, Jesse, Private, Contl. Line, 3 years' service.
Utterback, Benj., Private, State Line, 3 years' service.
Briscoe, Jno., Private, State Navy, 3 years' service.
Devier, John, Private, State Line, 3 years' service.
Foster, Jno., Private, Contl. Line, 3 years' service.
Stevens, Edwd., Brig.-Gen., Contl. Line, 3 years' service.
Melton, Isham, Private, State Line, 3 years' service.
Melton, John, Private, State Line, 3 years' service.
Elliott, Wm., Corporal, Contl. Line, 3 years' service.
Goodrum, Thos., Corporal, Contl. Line, 3 years' service.
Croghan, Wm., Major, Contl. Line, 7 years' service.
Newman, Owen, Sergeant, Contl. Line, 7 years' service.
Hawkins, Jas., Private, Contl. Line, 3 years' service.
Barton, Thos., Private, State Line, 3 years' service.
Allen, Edwd., Lieut., Contl. Line, 3 years' service.
Alman. Wm., Gunner, State Navy, 3 years' service.
Sandefer, Saml., Private, Contl. Line, 3 years' service.
Wren, Alex., Private, State Line, 3 years' service.
Matthews, Geo., Col., Contl. Line, 7 years' service.
Fitzgerald, Jas., Private, Contl. Line, 3 years' service.
Taylor, Reuben, Captain, Contl. Line, 3 years' service.
Taylor, Francis, Major, Contl. Line, 3 years' service.
Denton, Jno., Private, State Line, 3 years' service.
Hazlewood, Wm., Sergeant, State Line, 3 years' service.
King, Elisha, Lieut., Contl. Line, 3 years' service.
Lane, Zach., Private, State Line, 3 years' service.
Edwards, Enoch, Seaman, State Navy, 3 years' service.
Lawson, Robt., Brig.-Gen., Contl. Line, 3 years' service.
Pasteur, Bluitt, Seaman, State Navy, 3 years' service.
Pasley, Joel, Private, State Line, 3 years' service.
Scott, Jas., Private, Contl. Line, 3 years' service.
Lewis, Matt., Seaman, State Navy, 3 years' service.
Bushell, John, Private, Contl. Line, 3 years' service.
Jennings, Thos., Sailor, State Navy, 3 years' service.
Jennings, Wm., Sailor, State Navy, 3 years' service.
Jenkins, Rich., Private, Contl. Line, 3 years' service.
Leonard, Wm., Sailor, State Navy, 3 years' service.

Armestead, Wm., Private, State Line, 3 years' service.
Biscoe, Jas., Boatswain, State Navy, 3 years' service.
Whitfield, Haynes, Sailor, State Navy, 3 years' service.
Smith, Jno., Sailor, State Navy, 3 years' service.
Pigott, Abraham, Private, Contl. Line, 3 years' service.
Butty, Thos., Sailor, State Navy, 3 years' service.
Burk, Jas., Gunner, State Navy, 3 years' service.
Humphlett, Wm., Seaman, State Navy, 3 years' service.
Ballard, Wm., Pilot, State Navy, 3 years' service.
Whitletors, Levi, Private, Contl. Line, 3 years' service.
Edmundson, Rich., Sergeant, Contl. Line, 3 years' service.
Taliaferro, Wm., Lieut.-Col., Contl. Line, 3 years' service;
    issued to Wm. Taliaferro, representative of Lieut.-Col.
    Wm. Taliaferro.
Loyd, Geo., Sergeant, Contl. Line, 3 years' service.
Dawson, Francis, Sergeant, Contl. Line, 3 years' service.
Furbush, Wm., Sergeant, Contl. Line, 3 years' service.
Fauntleroy, Hy., Captain, Contl. Line, 3 years' service; war-
    rant issued to John, William, Moore, Griffin, Joseph
    and Robt. Fauntleroy, rep. of Capt. Hy. Fauntleroy.

EARLY SETTLERS IN VIRGINIA

Bushell, Nicholas, transported by John Upton, 7 July, 1635.
Butler, Joane, transported by Thomas Harwood, 7 July,
    1635.
Butler, William, transported by Christopher Branch of
    Henrico Co., 8 December, 1635.
Cary, William, transported by Miles Cary, gent., of York
    County, 7 November, 1700.
Carter, George, transported by Lieut. John Cheesman of
    Charles River County, 21 November, 1635.
Cason, Thomas, transported by Thomas Harwood, 7 July,
    1635.
Causey, John (servant), transported by William Berriman,
    6 August, 1635.
Champion, John, transported by Daniel Cugley, Accomac
    County, 25 June, 1635.
Castle, Joane, transported by Thomas Eyre of Accomac
    County, 7 November, 1700.
Chesheire, Robert, an Irishman (servant), transported by
    William Stone of Accomac County, 4 June, 1635.

Chilcott, Thomas (servant), transported by William Stone
of Accomac County, 4 June, 1635.

Clarke, George, transported by John Parrott, 24 May, 1635.

Clarke, John, transported by John Sparkes, 3 June, 1635.

Clarke, Nicholas (servant), transported by William Gany
of Accomac County, 17 September, 1635.

Clarke, Richard, transported by George Menifee, 2 July,
1635.

Calmore, Ralph, transported by Gideon Macon, gent., of
New Kent County, 7 November, 1700.

Carker, William, transported by William Montague of Mid-
dlesex County, 7 November, 1700.

Clayton, Thomas (servant), transported by William Spencer, 19 June, 1635.

Clement, John, transported by Jeremiah Clement, 11 June,
1635.

Clement, Margaret, transported by William Woolritch of
Elizabeth City, 17 June, 1635.

Clements, Jeremiah, Upper Chippooks Creek, son and heir
of Elizabeth Clements, deceased. The said Elizabeth,
her sons Jeremiah, Nicholas and Ezekiel and Elizabeth
Clements her daughter, all came in the "George" in
1611.

Cloyes, John, transported by John Moone, 21 October, 1635.

Cockshott, Edward, transported by Capt. William Peirce,
22 June, 1635.

Coffin, Francis, transported by Thomas Smith, 21 July,
1635.

Cole, John, transported by David Jones, 4 July, 1635.

Cartwright, Thomas, transported by William Major of New
Kent County, 7 November, 1700.

Cushen, Richard, transported by James Boughar, gent., of
King and Queen County, 7 November, 1700.

Cole, Richard, transported by John Sparkes, 3 June, 1635.

Cole, Thomas (servant), transported by Charles Harmar,
4 July, 1635.

Cole, William (servant), transported by William Cole of
Accomac County, 4 June, 1635.

Cole, William (servant), transported by William Gany of
Accomac County, 17 September, 1635.

Colling, Walter, transported by Thomas Bagwell, 7 November, 1635.

Collins, Giles, transported by Capt. Thomas Willoughby,
19 March, 1643.

204 VIRGINIA COUNTY RECORDS.

Collins, Henry, transported by Hugh Cox, 6 December, 1634.

Collins, John (servant), transported by William Gany of Accomac County, 17 September, 1635.

Collins, Thomas (servant), transported by William Gany of Accomac County, 17 September, 1635.

Colson, Susan, transported by Capt. Adam Thoroughgood in the "Hopewell" in 1628.

Combe, Richard, transported by Doctoris Christmas of Elizabeth City, 21 November, 1635.

Combey, Ann, transported by John Dennett, 10 August, 1635.

Carr, John, transported by James Boughar, gent., of King and Queen County, 7 November, 1700.

Cooke, Ann, transported by William Prior, 11 July, 1635.

Cooke, George (servant), transported by Thomas Davis in the "George" in 1617.

Cooper, Henry, transported by Capt. William Peirce, 21 July, 1635.

Cooper, John, transported by Henry Harte, 1 August, 1635.

Callaway, Cornelius, transported by Thomas Cooper of Nansemond County, 7 November, 1700.

Coplestone, Annanias (servant), transported by William Spencer, 19 June, 1635.

Corbett, Robert, transported by Lieut. John Cheesman of Charles River County, 21 November, 1635.

Costerdine, Francis, transported by William Clarke, 1 July, 1635.

Cotterell, Edward, transported by Lieut. John Cheesman, Charles River County, 21 November, 1635.

Cottle, Thomas, transported by John Parrott, 24 May, 1635.

Carson, Da., transported by Peter Massee of New Kent County, 7 November, 1700.

Courtney, James (servant), transported by Charles Harmar, 4 July, 1635.

Crabb, John, transported by Capt. Adam Thoroughgood, 18 December, 1635.

Clark, John, transported by Peter Massie of New Kent, 7 November, 1700.

Creason, Elizabeth, transported by Capt. Adam Thoroughgood, 24 June, 1635.

Crewe, Rebena (servant), transported by Joseph Johnson, 19 June, 1635.

Crofton, Thomas, transported by William Wilkinson, minister, 20 November, 1635.

Crocker, Pascall, transported by Daniel Cugley of Accomac, 25 June, 1635.

Croker, John, transported by Thomas Shippey, 14 November, 1635.

Cropp, Thomas (servant), transported by Capt. Francis Epes, 26 August, 1635.

Crosbye, Henry, transported by Hugh Cox, 6 December, 1634.

Crost, John, transported by William Barker, 26 November, 1635.

Cullembire, Richard, transported by Richard Bennett, 26 June, 1635.

Cullybrant, Sarah, transported by William Barker, 26 November, 1635.

Curtisse, Elizabeth, transported by Capt. Adam Thoroughgood, 24 June, 1635.

(To be continued)

Index to Vol. 7

Index